Present Values

This volume is about economists, economics, and issues of concern to Indian society. Some essays are expository, and some satirical. Together, they offer a commentary on the state of the discipline of economics today and on aspects of contemporary India's society and polity. The volume affords insights into, among other things,

- the pervasive influence of economists such as Kenneth Arrow and Anthony Atkinson, and thinkers such as Tom Paine, Jonathan Swift, and Dadabhai Naoroji;
- the place of markets and game theory (and even crime fiction!) in present-day economics;
- the affectations and convoluted mathematisation of a good deal of 'mainstream' economics; and
- India's recent political climate, and the conduct of various arms of the legislature, the executive, and the judiciary in the country.

Engaging and lucidly written, this volume should be of interest to scholars of economics, political science, development studies, South Asian studies, and, above all, the general reader.

S. Subramanian is a former Professor of Economics from the Madras Institute of Development Studies, India, and a former Indian Council of Social Science Research National Fellow. He has research interests in the fields of poverty, inequality, demography, welfare economics, social choice theory, and development economics. He is an elected Fellow of the Human Development and Capabilities Association and was a member of the advisory board of the World Bank's Commission on Global Poverty (2015–16). He is the author of, among other books, *Rights, Deprivation, and Disparity* (2006), *The Poverty Line* (2012), and *Inequality and Poverty: A Short Critical Introduction* (2019). He has published articles in a number of scholarly journals including the *Journal of Development Economics*, *Social Choice and Welfare*, *Mathematical Social Sciences*, *Theory and Decision*, and *Economic and Political Weekly*.

Present Values
Essays on Economics and
Aspects of Indian Society

S. Subramanian

LONDON AND NEW YORK

First published 2020
by Routledge
2 Park Square, Milton Park, Abingdon, Oxon OX14 4RN

and by Routledge
52 Vanderbilt Avenue, New York, NY 10017

Routledge is an imprint of the Taylor & Francis Group, an informa business

© 2020 S. Subramanian

The right of S. Subramanian to be identified as author of this work has been asserted by him in accordance with sections 77 and 78 of the Copyright, Designs and Patents Act 1988.

All rights reserved. No part of this book may be reprinted or reproduced or utilised in any form or by any electronic, mechanical, or other means, now known or hereafter invented, including photocopying and recording, or in any information storage or retrieval system, without permission in writing from the publishers.

Trademark notice: Product or corporate names may be trademarks or registered trademarks, and are used only for identification and explanation without intent to infringe.

British Library Cataloguing-in-Publication Data
A catalogue record for this book is available from the British Library

Library of Congress Cataloging-in-Publication Data
Names: Subramanian, S., author.
Title: Present values : essays on economics and aspects of Indian society / S. Subramanian.
Description: Milton Park, Abingdon, Oxon ; New York, NY : Routledge, 2020. | Includes bibliographical references.
Identifiers: LCCN 2020005595 (print) | LCCN 2020005596 (ebook)
Subjects: LCSH: Economics—India. | India—Economic conditions—1991–
Classification: LCC HB126.I4 S83 2020 (print) | LCC HB126.I4 (ebook) | DDC 330.0954—dc23
LC record available at https://lccn.loc.gov/2020005595
LC ebook record available at https://lccn.loc.gov/2020005596

ISBN: 978-0-367-48167-4 (hbk)
ISBN: 978-1-003-05032-2 (ebk)

Typeset in Times New Roman
by Apex CoVantage, LLC

Contents

Acknowledgements   vii

Introduction   1

PART I
On economics and economic themes, with some digressions   3

1. In memoriam: K. J. Arrow and A. B. Atkinson   5
2. Tom Paine, *Rights of Man*, and the foundations of the welfare state   8
3. Three themes in economics: the market, game theory, and famine   13
4. An economist's descent into crime   21

PART II
On some tendencies in the dismal science   27

5. Economics: the view from above   29
6. Hyman Kaplan and the G*L*O*B*A*L P*O*V*E*R*T*Y L*I*N*E   40
7. A Leacockian view of economics today   48

PART III
On institutions, culture, and society 57

8 Learning economics and the law anew 59
9 The adventures of 'Chalak' Om, as chronicled
   by Dr Vatsan 63
   ATHUR KANNAN THAYYIL

Index 81

Acknowledgements

The chapters in this book have been previously published and are here reprinted with minor alterations to the titles or other small editorial amendments. For permission to reproduce the articles, the author would like to thank the editors and publishers of the following publications: *The Tribune* (Chandigarh, India), *The New School Economic Review*, *Think: Philosophy for Everyone (Journal of the Royal Institute of Philosophy)*, *The Wire*, and *The Economic and Political Weekly*. Details regarding the original sources of publication are provided, for each relevant chapter, in what follows:

Chapter 1 (IN MEMORIAM: K. J. ARROW AND A. B. ATKINSON): 'A Salute to Great Economists,' *The Tribune, March 17, 2017.*

Chapter 2 (TOM PAINE, *RIGHTS OF MAN*, AND THE FOUNDATIONS OF THE WELFARE STATE): 'Revisiting "Natural Rights" of Man,' *The Tribune, February 19, 2016;* 'We Need a Robust Welfare State,' *The Tribune, March 4, 2016.*

Chapter 3 (THREE THEMES IN ECONOMICS: THE MARKET, GAME THEORY, AND FAMINE): 'The Market: In Theory, Fact, and Lore,' *The Tribune, June 20, 2016;* 'Game Theory: In Literature, Life, and Sport,' *The Tribune, September 2, 2016;* 'Drought and Entitlements: Two Classic Indictments of Famine,' *The Tribune, April 22, 2016.*

Chapter 4 (AN ECONOMIST'S DESCENT INTO CRIME): 'Profit Motive: Fiction and the Economics of Crime,' *The Tribune, August 5, 2016;* 'Enduring Appeal of the Locked Room Mystery,' *The Tribune, April 2, 2016.*

Chapter 5 (ECONOMICS: THE VIEW FROM ABOVE): 'The View from Above,' *Economic and Political Weekly: 50(14): April 4, 2015; 50(20): May 16, 2015; 50(29): July 18, 2015; 50(37): September 12, 2015; 50(41): October 10, 2015.*

viii *Acknowledgements*

Chapter 6 (HYMAN KAPLAN AND THE G*L*O*B*A*L P*O*V*E*R*T*Y L*I*N*E): 'Hyman Kaplan and the G*L*O*B*A*L P*O*V*E*R*T*Y L*I*N*E,' *Think: Philosophy for Everyone (Journal of the Royal Institute of Philosophy), 15(42): 91–102, 2016.*

Chapter 7 (A LEACOCKIAN VIEW OF ECONOMICS TODAY): 'A Leacockian View of Economics Today,' *The New School Economic Review, 9(1): 29–37*, 2017.

Chapter 8 (LEARNING ECONOMICS AND THE LAW ANEW): 'Vedanomics is All We Need for Acche Din,' *The Wire, March 25, 2018*; 'Justice for All, Comprehension for None,' *The Wire, July 6, 2018.*

Chapter 9 (THE ADVENTURES OF 'CHALAK' OM, AS CHRONICLED BY DR VATSAN): 'The Adventures of "Chalak" Om, As Chronicled by Dr Vatsan,' *The Wire: December 30, 2018; January 13, 2019; January 22, 2019; February 3, 2019.*

Introduction

> History started badly and hav been getting steadily worse.
> —Nigel Molesworth in Geoffrey Willans's *Down With Skool!* (1953)

There is a rumour to the effect that economists are not really human, but rather robots, or aliens, or, worse still, zombies. I am in no position to comment on these speculations while still preserving myself from the risk of betraying the tribe to which I belong. Having said this, I wonder if I may advance the possibility that the members of this species may actually be androids infected by certain production defects which occasionally make them human in unexpected ways, that is to say, capable of saying nice things about others, of taking the trouble of explaining their esoteric theories to those that do not speak their language, of reading detective stories, of taking a squiggle-eyed view of their own work and that of their colleagues, and of sometimes taking a break from their grim-death view of the world in favour of actually finding something funny about the universe they inhabit. This book is a very small collection of previously published essays that reflect the stated aberrant-humanoid view of the dismal scientist.

The book is divided into three parts. The first is 'On Economists and Economic Themes, with Some Digressions.' It begins with a heartfelt celebration of two great contemporary economists who are no longer in our midst: Kenneth J. Arrow and Anthony B. Atkinson. The next chapter is again a tribute, on this occasion to the great revolutionary Tom Paine and the continuing relevance of his book *Rights of Man* for a humane striving after a just and democratic society and economy. This is followed by two essentially expository pieces on certain themes in mainstream economics: those of the market and of game theory and a review of two classic treatments of the phenomenon of famine, as reflected in Jonathan Swift's 'modest proposal' and Dadabhai Naoroji's indictment of 'un-British rule in India.' The final essay in Part I is a complete holiday from the customary solemnity of economic analyses and is devoted to an exploration of why economic theorists might conceivably entertain a yen for crime novels.

The second part of the book ('On Some Tendencies in the Dismal Science') is a satirical take on certain affectations of mainstream economics. The essays here are an 'insider's' parodies of the discipline, and the author is not exempt from his own criticisms of the solemnity of the subject, its ponderousness and convoluted mathematisation, the magisterial pronouncements of its practitioners, and their unwillingness to acknowledge that it is their ideology that frequently produces their 'science.'

The final part of the book ('On Institutions, Culture, and Society') is a set of spoofs on the conduct of various arms of the legislature, the executive, and the judiciary in India in recent times. It reviews the parlous state to which this country has been reduced through an approach to governance constituted by right-wing religious extremism, communal majoritarianism, discord in our law courts, and the suborning and corruption of the institutions of administration. The essays in Parts II and III of the book are intended to be cautionary notices against the vices of disciplinary parochialism and nationalistic chauvinism. They may occasionally come across as being bitter and cynical in tone, although it may be more helpful to see them as a gruff defence of elements of humane scepticism, inspired by involvement rather than petulance. In any event, that is not for me to judge.

It remains to end this introduction with an acknowledgement. The pieces assembled in this book were earlier published in the Chandigarh-based *Tribune*, in *The Economic and Political Weekly*, in *The Wire*, in *The New School Economic Review*, and in *Think: Philosophy for Everyone (Journal of the Royal Institute of Philosophy)*. I am indebted to the editors who presided over these publications at the time I wrote for them. For giving me frequent opportunities to find a platform for my views, I would especially like to thank Dr Harish Khare, Dr Rammanohar Reddy, and Dr Siddharth Varadarajan. Finally, I owe many thanks to Aakash Chakrabarty of Routledge for his excellent editorial guidance in the preparation of this book.

Part I
On economics and economic themes, with some digressions

1 In memoriam

K. J. Arrow and A. B. Atkinson

Notes for the reader

This essay is a tribute to the learning, the genius, and the endearing human qualities of two very great economists of the last century and the present one.

2017 witnessed the passing of two extraordinary figures in the world of economics. Sir Anthony Barnes Atkinson (1944–2017) passed away on New Year's Day, at the relatively early age of 72, after a battle with cancer; and Kenneth Joseph Arrow (1921–2017) passed away on February 21st, at the age of 95. This article is a brief commemoration of these two outstanding contributors to the realm of economic ideas.

Arrow's work in economics is so seminal and so wide-ranging that he must be regarded as one of the first among equals in the list of those that have shaped the discipline. His research (in a space-saving exiguous catalogue) covers the fields of welfare economics, social choice theory, general equilibrium analysis, the economics of risk and uncertainty, and the economics of asymmetric information, not to mention work in econometric theory. It is impossible to avoid bumping into Arrow, no matter what area of economics one considers. Thus it is that we have (in another deliberately skimpy list) the Arrow Impossibility Theorem; Arrow's Extended Sympathy; the Arrow-Debreu Model of General Equilibrium; the Arrow-Pratt Measures of Risk-Aversion; the Arrow Model of Health Insurance and Market Failure; and the Arrow-Chenery-Minhas-Solow Production Function. In 1972, Arrow was awarded the Nobel Prize in Economics – he is the youngest person, at the age of 51, to receive the honour. For the larger part of his academic career, Arrow was associated with Stanford University, and with three of its Departments – those of Economics, Operations Research, and Philosophy.

For a mathematical economist credited with importing formidable standards of formal rigour and technical finesse into economics, Arrow took a broad and humane view of the subject, which found ample space for both philosophy and poetry in his reckoning of it. Thus, in his 1971 book on General Competitive Analysis, written with another mathematical economist, Frank Hahn of Cambridge, we find an ironic reference to the Standard

6 *On economics and economic themes*

Model of Rational Economic Man in the form of a fragment from a poem of W. B. Yeats:

> A levelling, rancorous, rational sort of mind
> That never looked out of the eye of a saint
> Or out of drunkard's eye.

Another example of Arrow's capacious catholicity is to be found in the inspiration for his rigorously conceived view of 'extended sympathy' as a form of ordinal interpersonal comparison of utilities: he discovered this inspiration, during a visit to England, in a 17th century tombstone bearing this inscription:

> Here lies Martin Engelbrodde,
> Ha'e mercy on my soul, Lord God,
> As I would do were I Lord God,
> And Thou wert Martin Engelbrodde.

It is typical of Arrow that he translated this sentiment into the formulation $(x,i)\tilde{P}(y,j)$.

Atkinson, like Arrow, was a rigorous economic theorist, who started out studying Mathematics before switching to Economics, and was much influenced by the earlier-mentioned economist Sir Frank Hahn, at Cambridge, where Atkinson did his undergraduate degree. He is one of the few very great contemporary academics who never did a Ph.D. He is also one of the greatest modern economists – along, I would say, with Piero Sraffa, Joan Robinson, and Serge-Christophe Kolm – who was never awarded the Nobel Prize (a discredit to the Nobel Committee that is only compounded by some of the wholly undeserving names that have made it to the Nobel Laureates' list). Atkinson's name will be inextricably linked with the subjects of inequality and poverty. He wrote at least two path-breaking journal articles: one (published in *The Journal of Economic Theory* in 1970) was titled 'On the Measurement of Inequality'; and the other (published in *Econometrica* in 1987) was titled 'On the Measurement of Poverty.' If he had written nothing else, these two essays between them would have served to account for a life-time's work. Atkinson, at the end of his career, was Centennial Professor at the London School of Economics, and Senior Research Fellow at Nuffield College, Oxford.

The details of Arrow's and Atkinson's scientific contributions can be found in Wikipedia, among other sources. Here, I would like to share a couple of personal reminiscences that reflect both the extraordinary and the human-size features of their character. (If there is some suspicion that

I am about to engage in a bit of name-dropping, then the suspicion is well-founded: I am not too proud to say that I feel deeply privileged to have had the opportunity, in my lifetime, of being associated with these gentlemen, however briefly and tangentially.) I have met Arrow just once. This was in the mid-1980s when Arrow was a guest of the Delhi School of Economics, and I was visiting that institution then. The economist P. R. Brahmananda, who claimed to possess some astrological skills, was present on the occasion, and he insisted on reading Arrow's palm in which he said he detected 'two stars,' of which one had already been realized. Arrow chuckled and said the first star must be the Nobel, and he hoped the second star didn't mean another Nobel was on the way – one was quite enough. During a quiet moment that evening I asked Arrow if the suggestion that he had cracked the Arrow Theorem in just three weeks, when he was still a Ph.D. student, was a true story or an apocryphal one. Arrow leant forward with a grin, and said in a confidential whisper: 'Apocryphal, actually. Actually, it took me only two days. The first day, I proved that the result held for triples. After a disturbed night's sleep, on the following morning, I generalized the result.'

Atkinson, like Arrow, was a simple, direct person, whose humility showed through his soft-spoken conversation. I once shared a long walk with him on the evening of a conference held in the city of Viterbo, not far from Rome. Somehow the conversation turned to the famously eccentric Cambridge don Frank Hahn (mentioned earlier) who had been a considerable influence on Atkinson in the latter's student days. Atkinson recalled wryly that on the occasion when he first met Hahn, the latter opened the door to his knock and confided that he had been told to expect Atkinson who, Hahn added he had been informed, wasn't quite the idiot he looked. . . . I had the great good fortune of working with Atkinson as a member of the Advisory Board of the World Bank-appointed Commission on Global Poverty. Atkinson was Chairman of the Commission, and the Report which he authored, as Chairman, was the last significant piece of work he did, toward the end of 2016. It is a heroic record of work, conducted against the impossible odds of his illness, and requiring him to balance the views of 23 other scholars on the Advisory Board, while finding a place in the Report for his own convictions and predilections. Like the man, the Report was firm, frank, principled, and polite: critical of the World Bank, but without carrying a sledgehammer to the criticism.

In the generally bleak intellectual and moral environment in which professional thinkers these days often find themselves subsisting, it is nice to be able to say, of persons like Kenneth Arrow and Tony Atkinson, that these were not only great, but also very good, men.

2 Tom Paine, *Rights of Man*, and the foundations of the welfare state

Notes for the reader

This essay presents a broad-brush picture of one of the great thinkers and social reformers in the history of ideas: Tom Paine—citizen, political analyst, promoter and defender of human rights, economic analyst, and in many ways a pioneer in the field of social welfare provisioning in the modern state.

The man

In the times and circumstances and the countries in which many of us live, what can be more germane to a contemplation of those aspects of polity and economy which shape human welfare than the subjects of human rights, society and civilisation, the substantive forms of government—hereditary and representative—, constitutionalism, democracy, religion and the state, capital punishment, war, debt, trade, public spending, taxation, and social security? These are the themes which some of our public intellectuals are continuously engaged in, each with her or his own subject of special interest and competence, while other public intellectuals downplay their importance in the scheme of things with opinions that either neglect or debase the themes.

Nothing very much would seem to have changed in the debates—except perhaps their quality—that informed the two great revolutions which the world witnessed over two hundred years ago: the American War of Independence of 1776, and the French Revolution of 1787. These debates culminated in the publication, in 1792, of one of the world's great classics of reason and morality, Tom Paine's *Rights of Man*, which covered the entire breadth of the themes sketched out above, with a felicity of language, passion of feeling, simplicity of expression, and directness of logic that is unsurpassed, in the opinion of many, for the virtues of genius, lucidity, and principle that it reflects.

Tom Paine was an Englishman by birth, and a citizen of the world by profession. A man who came to acquire an overwhelming passion for freedom matched only by his detestation of despotism, Paine travelled to the New World to participate in America's war against his own country of birth, and contributed richly to the ideas which animated that struggle, in the company of such men of distinction associated with America's independence as George Washington, Benjamin Franklin, and Thomas Jefferson. This should have been sufficient testimony to any single, quite extraordinary, human being's allegiance to his principles, but Paine went further: pursuing a friendship conceived during the American struggle with the Frenchman La Fayette, he participated in the ensuing French Revolution as well, and was in a position to turn in an eyewitness's account of the taking of the Bastille.

The French Revolution provoked fear and antipathy amongst monarchists across Europe, and one of the most celebrated tracts against France's successful struggle was contained in the book *Reflections on the Revolution of France* by Edmund Burke, a man known for that stirring paean to reactionary sentiment which still routinely finds its way into the great quotations of literature: 'The age of chivalry is gone. That of sophisters, economists and calculators has succeeded; and the glory of Europe is extinguished forever.' Burke's tract served as an occasion for Paine's repudiation of the canons of conservative thought embodied in it, and *Rights of Man*, while directed against Burke's *Reflections*, served as a much larger canvas for an exploration of those ideas in political philosophy and public morality which, with the ushering in of a new order as in America and France, cried out for systematic analysis and presentation. Paine's great work struck a chord in the hearts of Englishmen of ordinary rank, and the book sold thousands upon thousands of copies, to the chagrin of the aristocrats who banked erroneously on Burke's book appealing to a wide readership.

The book

Rights of Man is a book in two parts. Part 1 begins with a repudiation of Burke that is at once clever and cogent, clinical and mocking. A stirring account is offered of the events leading up to the taking of the Bastille, as a corrective to what Paine perceives to be Burke's calumnies upon the French Revolution. These specific events are placed in the larger context of the principles underlying the revolution—and focused on the primacy of the rights of man—a notion which the jurist and philosopher Jeremy Bentham (the intellectual father of the system called Utilitarianism) dismissed as 'nonsense upon stilts.' Nothing deterred, Paine upholds the sanctity of what he calls the 'natural' rights of man (subsequently encoded as human rights in the United Nations' lexicon), and distinguishes these from civil rights which are reposed by the individual in society as a part of a social compact by which society provides those arrangements that enable the transformation of formal entitlements into substantive realisations.

These considerations lead naturally to questions about the form of government which is compatible with an acknowledgement of the rights of man. Paine dissects and casts aside monarchical or aristocratic or hereditary government (and his observations on dynastic rule are relevant even today in many countries, when changes in form may leave behind no changes in the essence of the governance system). The notion of representative government is introduced and commended; and the place of equality and democracy in government premised upon the existence of inalienable human rights is emphasised. But prior even to a government so conceived is the requirement of a well-defined constitution, such as the Americans and the French gave to themselves, unlike the British who had to content themselves with the Magna Carta, a poor parody, in Paine's view, of a genuine constitution.

In Part 2, Paine turns from France to America, describes the founding principles of that nation, and extols the virtues of representative government as the only form of government that will deliver democracy in extensive and populous societies (in distinction to the 'simple democracy' of ancient Athenian society). His reflections on parliamentary democracy—a social arrangement of recent vintage which we take for granted and whose degeneration we often fail to register on our consciousness—are fascinating. This 'new' form of government is contrasted with the 'old' form, one which draws its sustenance from 'war and extortion.'

In a deep and brilliant series of analyses for the betterment of the civilisations of Europe and America, Paine expounds on how debt and strife keep out human development (as they do today in some of the poorest nations of the world); on how rational government requires the separation of Church from State (an outcome far removed from the theocratic ambitions of many States today); on the true meaning of toleration and intolerance (which should make us cringe when contrasted with the notions often peddled by the ruling classes of many countries in the contemporary world); and on the obligations of a civilised and (civilising) State toward the poor and the dispossessed (as much observed in the breach in many parts of the world today as in Paine's natal country then).

In the course of time, every great work of the mind achieves, as the writer James Agee put it, 'emasculation by acceptance.' *Rights of Man* is no exception, not least when its precepts and ambitions are set against the tokenistic lip-service paid to good governance today in many countries of the world. For contrast a great deal of contemporary reality with Tom Paine's moving expectation in the world around him: '. . . nothing of reform in the political world ought to be held improbable. It is an age of

Revolutions, in which everything may be looked for.' Looked for, we may add, but all too often not found! This is nowhere truer than in the context of the welfare state.

Social security and skewed priorities

Paine, who today would carry the labels of political philosopher, economist, and activist but in his time was more familiarly known simply as a pamphleteer, laid the groundwork for a system of social security for the poor over 230 years ago in *Rights of Man*. He dealt at length with a set of government policies which in his view would conduce to the betterment of Europe and America. The policies he dealt with related, among other things, to measures aimed at cooperative disarmament, the accommodation of religious plurality in a diverse society, the freeing up of trade both domestic and international, amelioration of the national debt, mitigation of the harsher aspects of taxation, the rationalisation and 'humanisation' of the pattern of public spending, and the provision of protection to the poor of the nation. These meditations of Paine bespeak a mind capable of the profoundest rationality, modernity, common sense, and moral reasoning.

His views on social security and the welfare state, in particular, are a marvel of prescience: they anticipate the UN's subsequent championing of specific measures of promotional and protective social security measures, founded on a view of social and economic human rights.

Paine's strictures against a monarchic government's policy of employing the national exchequer to enrich the landed aristocracy at the expense of the poor continue to find relevance today—but in the distressing context of representative, not monarchic, government! Country-specific statistics on budgetary allocations for social sector spending, on allocations for indirect and direct tax concessions to the corporate sector, and on the quantum of stressed loans and non-productive assets (largely accounted for by corporate borrowings) in the banking sector, are compatible with an assessment of Paine's, made in the context of England in 1792, that '. . . were an estimation to be made of the charge of Aristocracy to a Nation, it will be found nearly equal to that of supporting the poor' (*Rights of Man*).

It is instructive to consider Paine's meticulous rewriting of England's budgetary dispositions for the year 1787. He confines himself to current spending on items other than debt retirement—a sum of some 7.5 million shillings, devoted largely to the upkeep of the landed gentry through a harsh and regressive system of indirect and direct taxes. In his altered composition of government spending, Paine recommends that annual expenditures for the administration of government and the upkeep of the armed forces should be of the order of 1.5 million shillings; that a further million shillings should be spent on soldiers and sailors to be disbanded over time from the army and the navy in the cause of a leaner armed force; that a million shillings be retained for other contingencies, through the abolition of certain regressive taxes and the institution of an ingenious system of progressive land taxation; and that as much as four million shillings be earmarked for social security provisioning, of which fully two million would be financed by a wholesale remission of the so-called Poor Taxes that were levied on parish properties under the Poor Laws of England and Wales, and two million through the abolition of other taxes on the poor.

Paine has a detailed guide for the apportionment of social spending under different heads—by way of support for poor families based on a stipulated rate for each child under 14 years of age; support for the education of children from poor or not-quite-affluent families; old-age allowances, at different rates for those between the ages of 50 and 60, and those over the age of 60 (including poor widows); allowances to the poor for births, marriages, and funerals; and unemployment relief. Paine's computations have the appearance of back-of-the envelope calculations, but are actually based on ingenious estimates of the sizes of different categories of the population, pointing to an impressive deployment of actuarial and demographic arithmetic.

Then, now, and Tom Paine's query

Paine's budgetary calculations suggest a pattern of spending from the pubic exchequer of England in 1787 in which at least 53 per cent of total spending is for the poor. In our own contemporary budgets, social sector spending is often less than a quarter of the total outlay. Of this spending, in many countries, much is frittered away through inefficiency, negligence, and outright theft (an unholy trinity that travels under the polite alias of 'leakages'). And now, the tendency is for many governments to retreat even further from responsible social sector engagement through privatisation, or principles of 'ability to pay,' or throwing cash at the poor. There is good case for our being moved to shame and stirred to anger when we set the welfare-related performance of many of our states today against Paine's question, posed thus in *Rights of Man*:

> is it, then, better that the lives of one hundred and forty thousand aged persons be rendered comfortable, or that a million a year of public money be expended on any one individual, and him often of the most worthless or insignificant character? Let reason and justice, let honour and humanity, let even hypocrisy, sycophancy and Mr Burke, let George, let Louis, Leopold, Frederic, Catherine, Cornwallis, or Tipoo Saib, answer the question.

3 Three themes in economics
The market, game theory, and famine

Notes for the reader

The present chapter is essentially an exposition of certain salient themes in economics, and is intended as an introduction, for the non-specialist reader, to the subjects of the market in economic analysis, game theory, and two classic indictments of the phenomenon of famine by two persons who, without qualifying for the strict label of 'economists', nevertheless contributed profoundly to the discipline.

The market: in theory, fact, and lore

For proponents of the market as the finest—if not the only—institution that can guide a society to the best of all possible worlds, its virtues are legion, and the stuff of which mythologies are made. These virtues include attributes whose precise meaning is seldom clear—either to the advertiser of the virtues or his intended audience. It is thus often put out, in a vague sort of way, that the market, unlike other institutions (in particular the government), is 'efficient' and also 'fair.' Pressed for amplification, 'efficiency' in the mouth of the word's user—it often turns out—means something such as that cash transactions might be expected to be disposed of quicker in private-sector banks than in public-sector banks; or that 'fairness' could mean anything from 'equitableness' in the distribution of the national dividend to a system of rewards according to merit or desert. More precise advertisers of the market's virtues—economists and philosophers among them—will of course employ terms such as 'efficiency' and 'fairness' with greater care. They would suggest, for example, that the market will ensure the emergence of economic outcomes which are such that no one can be made better off without making someone else worse off, and that each factor of production (labour, capital) will receive a share of the economy's aggregate output according to that factor's marginal contribution to the creation of the output. These supposed virtues of the market are a part of its proponents' lore; and whether they are catalogued with greater or lesser precision, they constitute a shared belief of its functioning among the market's defenders, whether these defenders be laypersons or economists or philosophers or just plain ideologues.

If this is the market in lore, what is it like in fact? Often enough it is indeed the case that inter-State bus travel in India is quicker and more comfortable in a transport service provided by a private agency than if one were to depend on vehicles plied by the Public Transport Corporation (PTC) of one's State. Anecdotal examples such as this are often considered to constitute clinching evidence of the virtues of the market. What the evidence does not take account of, however, is the fact that State-subsidized PTCs make bus travel more affordable for poor passengers than commercial for-profit travel agencies; that PTCs will typically ply their vehicles through commercially unattractive routes in order to maximize the coverage of the need to which they cater; and that PTC vehicles will stop at more frequent intervals for exactly the same reason. The market, in fact, is often enough more unlike than like the market in lore. The allegedly superior informational and enforcement advantages enjoyed by the private banking sector are frequently reflected in loan recovery procedures that are distinguished only for their violent, strong-arm tactics. The global financial crisis of 2008 was triggered in the United States by an unregulated, freely-functioning private banking sector subjected to extremely lax public oversight. It is an ostensibly 'free' market which has played havoc with the prices of essential life-saving drugs, keeping the prevention and cure of life-threatening disease conditions effectively and forever beyond the reach of poor consumers. It is in market-driven capitalist economies such as the U.S. that economic inequality threatens to become a major factor in the de-stabilization of a society's cohesiveness: after outstanding work on the subject by economists like Stiglitz, Piketty, Atkinson, and Milanovic, the question of the continued sustainability of rising inequality can no longer be ignored by the world.

The virtues broadcast by the lore of the market are frequently, and unjustly, laid at the door of the theory of the market; and as for the facts of the market, these are often moulded out of recognition to fit the theory, in a heroic bid to force Life into an imitation of Art. The 'informal' understanding of the theory underlying the market's supposed virtues is to be found in Adam Smith's account of the Invisible Hand of private rationality and self-interest which, it is suggested, leads to a spontaneous order of collective optimality, in which economic allocations are arranged in such a way that an improvement in any one person's welfare can only be achieved at the cost of reducing some other person's welfare. (This outcome has subsequently been characterized as 'Pareto efficiency,' after the Italian sociologist Vilfredo Pareto.) Private egotism, in this view, will lead to public beneficence. It has taken years of hard analytical work in the fields of Welfare Economics and General Equilibrium Theory to distil this piece of folk wisdom into something like a set of formal propositions in terms of which the 'Invisible Hand' account of the economy could make sense. The First Theorem of Welfare Economics states that, *under certain well-defined conditions*, a *competitive equilibrium*, namely a set of market prices under which aggregate demand and aggregate supply will be perfectly balanced in an environment in which no agent is 'big' enough to influence prices by herself, will be Pareto efficient. There is no suggestion that such an equilibrium will be equitable or just. Indeed, the Second Theorem of Welfare Economics makes it clear that the equitableness of the competitive equilibrium will depend profoundly on the equitableness of the initial endowment of goods and services among the economy's agents.

Regrettably, both proponents and opponents alike of the market have tended to ignore the nuances of this theoretical work. Typically, proponents tend to gloss over the precise conditions under which the First Theorem holds. These conditions would include the empirically unlikely contingencies of an absence of 'externality' (which requires that individual consumption and production decisions are unaffected by the actions of others), and the availability of perfect and symmetric information about both the future and the quality of products transacted in the market. Opponents of the market tend to treat theory as apologetics for the market, as an elaborate and arcane system of mathematical mumbo-jumbo erected in order to protect the imagined virtues of the market in an impenetrable armour of logical formalisms. As it happens, theory is the most effective pointer to the limitations of the market. This is skilfully demonstrated by Anjan Mukherjee, a distinguished former professor of the Jawaharlal Nehru University (JNU), in an essay titled 'Market Failures: Almost Always?,' written in honour of another distinguished former professor of the JNU, Satish Jain, in a book titled *Themes in Economic Analysis* (Routledge, 2016). Mukherjee shows that asymmetric information can threaten the very existence of a competitive equilibrium, while externalities can threaten its efficiency. Ironically, it might require suitable regulatory action from government, or/and appropriately 'moral' behaviour from agents which departs from the standard model of egotistic individual rationality, to get the market to deliver. This is paradoxical, given the mental apparatus of General Equilibrium Theory's typical 'rational agent,' which two of its finest exponents, Kenneth Arrow and Frank Hahn, characterized in terms borrowed from the poetry of William Butler Yeats: 'A levelling, rancorous, rational sort of mind / That never looked out of the eye of a saint / Or out of drunkard's eye.'

As for our own economy, we have no cause for complaint: it is a just and impartial mix of market failure *and* government failure.

16   *On economics and economic themes*

Game theory: in literature, life, and sport

One of the intriguing things about a social science like Economics is how with the passage of time, heterodoxy can become orthodoxy, and orthodoxy heterodoxy. A major case in point is that of the behavioural foundations of economics, as reflected most sharply in the perceived relationship between private virtues (vices) and public vices (virtues). The apparent paradox of uncoordinated selfish individual actions leading to collective beneficence is well-captured in Adam Smith's account of the Invisible Hand, as encapsulated in that famous statement from *The Wealth of Nations*: 'It is *not* from the benevolence of the *butcher*, the brewer, or the *baker* that we expect our dinner, but from their regard to their own interest.' As it happens, Smith's sentiment in his 1776 book was preceded, in literature, by a similar viewpoint expressed by Bernard de Mandeville in his 1714 book *The Fable of the Bees, or, Private Vices, Publick Benefits*.

De Mandeville's book assumed the form of a poem (followed by a prose commentary) about a hive of bees—industrious, prosperous, and corrupt—that longed for the virtue of honesty which, when the wish was granted, however, led to contentment and lack of ambition among the bees, and so to the eventual dissolution of the hive. The saga is traced in verses such as these, describing first the initial nature of the hive, then how it is transformed by virtue, and eventually the moral to be learnt from the fable: 'Millions endeavouring to supply / Each other's Lust and Vanity . . . / Thus every Part was full of Vice, / Yet the whole Mass a Paradise . . . / For many Thousand Bees were lost. / Hard'ned with Toils, and Exercise / They counted Ease itself a Vice; / Which so improved their Temperance; / That, to avoid Extravagance, / They flew into a hollow Tree, Blest with Content and Honesty . . . Bare Virtue can't make Nations live / In Splendor; they, that would revive / A Golden Age, must be as free, / For Acorns, as for Honesty.'

The *Fable of the Bees* was received with shocked and scandalized disapproval. But Adam Smith's 'Invisible Hand' account of the economy eventually came to become the major orthodoxy of mainstream Neo-Classical Theory, as reflected in the micro-economics of General Competitive Equilibrium; and de Mandeville's views found expression in the macro-economic tenet of 'the paradox of thrift,' which suggests that saving (as opposed to spending) might be a private virtue, but one which can lead to public vice in the form of an inadequately stimulated economy.

In course of time, the old view that 'private greed and private rationality' is compatible with collectively sub-optimal outcomes again gained credence, through developments in the mathematics and economics of game theory. The archetypal formulation of the proposition is in terms of a problem called 'The Prisoner's Dilemma' (PD), which was discovered by two researchers, Melvin Dresher and Merrill Flood, at the Rand Corporation in the U.S., and formalized by Albert Tucker, a Princeton University mathematician. Here is one way of presenting the PD. Imagine two prisoners suspected of a crime who are interrogated in separate cells. Each can either confess to the crime or not confess. If both confess, both will receive a sentence of 5 years. If only one confesses, the confessor will be let off free for his honesty and the non-confessor will receive a sentence of 10 years for a crime compounded by lying. What should each prisoner do? If prisoner A confesses, prisoner B is best off also confessing (as that way B will receive 5 years rather than 10). If prisoner A does not confess, again prisoner B is best off confessing (as that way B will be let off rather than receive 5 years). Prisoner B's '*dominant strategy*' is, therefore, to confess. Prisoner A might be expected to reason in identical fashion, so that *his* dominant strategy will also be to confess. Thus both will end up confessing, drawing a sentence of 5 years each, when both might have been better off if only each had chosen the 'do not confess' strategy. When people behave strategically, private greed and private rationality can lead to social outcomes that are worse for all concerned parties than what they might have been in the presence of 'cooperative' rather than 'non-cooperative' individual behaviour.

The paradigm of the Prisoner's Dilemma contributes to an understanding of a number of real-life phenomena involving private strategies and public outcomes—for example: the non-observance of traffic rules; dishonest revelations of preference for public goods (recall the famous Akbar-and-Birbal story in which private rationality dictated that each citizen should contribute water to a well intended for the public collection of milk); deterrent stockpiling of weapons and the international arms race; the tragedy of the commons (over-grazing of commonly-owned pasture land); over-fishing of the seas; the functioning of market cartels and their frequent break-down. In each case, it is the relevant dominant-strategy equilibrium that is to blame.

At the heart of the problem is Yossarian's reasoning in Joseph Heller's famous novel of black humour, *Catch-22*. "'[Yossarian said:] From now on I'm thinking only of me." Major Danby replied indulgently with a superior smile: "But, Yossarian, suppose everyone felt that way." "Then," said Yossarian, "I'd certainly be a damned fool to feel any other way, wouldn't I?"' And, of course, Yossarian would be an even bigger damned fool to feel any other way if *nobody* felt that way! This, then, is precisely what paves the way for selfishness to be the dominant strategy equilibrium.

There are situations in which there may be no 'best' strategy available to any of the players in a game. A 'Nash Equilibrium' (named after the famous mathematician John Nash) of a game is one in which there is a combination of player-strategies such that, in this combination, each player's strategy is the best response by her, *given* the strategies of all the other players.

18 *On economics and economic themes*

Unfortunately, there are game-like situations in which there may not exist any Nash Equilibrium at all. This was literally true of a situation that arose in a cricket Test match between Australia and England. Denis Compton was batting for England, and he lofted the ball over the in-field whenever the Australian captain Don Bradman brought his fielders in, and tapped the ball for singles and twos when the opposing captain spread the field out. Compton says in his autobiography that Bradman became eventually so frustrated that he told Compton: 'This isn't cricket!'

If this episode had happened some years later and Bradman had been an economist or a mathematician, he might have been less judgemental and just said, matter-of-factly: 'This is a game without a ruddy Nash Equilibrium!' (Or 'gyme,' given that Bradman was Australian.)

Two classic indictments of famine

Even as drought hits the State of Maharashtra,[1] and other parts of the country, one is compellingly reminded of that great scourge of our colonial past: famine. In contemporary economics, we owe it to Amartya Sen for having brought this issue back into the domain of relevant discourse through his book, published in 1981, on *Poverty and Famines*. Sen provided detailed empirical accounts of the Bengal Famine of 1943–44, the Chinese famine during The Great Leap Forward in the late 1950s and the early 1960s, and the famines of the 1970s in Bangladesh and in Ethiopia.

The great value of Sen's work, apart from its obvious historical and empirical significance, lies in the theoretical framework which he employed to explicate the phenomenon of a certain type of famine. My reference is to his notion of '*entitlements,*' which determine the final consumption of goods and services—or just 'food' in the context of relevance here—which a person is able to achieve. How much food an individual or household is able to command would depend on the individual's initial endowment of 'wealth' (including 'assets' and labour-power); on the technology of production available whereby endowments can be converted into output for self-consumption or exchange in the market; on the terms of exchange, which are mediated by prices and wages; and by the legal framework, and its implementation, that circumscribe the means of access to final output. These factors, together, define one's *entitlements*. There are circumstances in which the factors can conspire to ensure that one's entitlement to food is insufficient to escape starvation; and famines are often the consequence of generalized and large-scale entitlement-failures.

Entitlement-failure, as Sen pointed out, can happen without 'Food Availability Decline.' That is to say, a famine is not necessarily caused by an aggregate supply deficiency of food: as Sen puts it, starvation can happen not because of there not *being* enough food to go around but because of some people not *having* adequate access to it. This could happen for a number of reasons: a sudden decline in endowments (such as loss of livestock in a pastoralist economy); or a sudden fall in wages because of deficiency of aggregate demand; or a sudden rise in the price of foodgrains (such as happened during the Bengal Famine because of the surge in demand for foodgrains caused by the war effort). It is not just in the matter of famine, or other 'natural' disasters, but also in the ordinary run of economic vicissitudes, that 'entitlement theory' is of assistance in focusing attention on those most vulnerable to entitlement-failure, namely the poor and the dispossessed.

A free press and parliamentary democracy have been found to be effective deterrents to large-scale famine. This is easily discernible from India's pre- and post-Independence records of famine. It is also evident in the great Irish famine of 1845–50, which was foreseen more than a century earlier in Jonathan Swift's savagely satirical indictment of the British government's heartless indifference to the plight of starving Irish folk. In 1729, the author of *Gulliver's Travels* published the tract titled 'A Modest Proposal for Preventing the Children of Poor People in Ireland, from Being a Burden on their Parents or Country, and for Making Them Beneficial to the Publick'—now known simply and famously as 'A Modest Proposal.' Swift's horrifyingly modest proposal was that poor Irish parents should sell their infants, when the latter reached the age of one year, at ten shillings an infant, to landlords, in the cause of the latter's consumption of '. . . a most delicious, nourishing and wholesome Food, whether Stewed, Roasted, Baked, or Boyled, [which] . . . will equally serve as a Fricasie, or Ragout.' Why landlords? Because 'I grant this food will be somewhat dear, and therefore very proper for Landlords, who, as they have already devoured most of the Parents, seem to have the best Title to the Children.' Swift proceeds to advance the merits of his proposal by pointing out, in the darkest of humours, that selling their children will relieve their parents of deprivation both through the proceeds of the sale and the cessation of the need to provide for them; and thus serve to reduce the incidence of both destitution and beggary, so distasteful in the eyes of the rich. Additionally, this would be a good way, Swift suggests, of checking the excess fertility of Catholics.

A different, and more passionately direct, indictment of a callous government is contained in the tract titled *Poverty and Un-British Rule in India*, by that great Indian nationalist Dadabhai Naoroji (1825–1917): Professor of Mathematics in Elphinstone College, Bombay; Professor of Gujarati in University College, London; Founder-Member-President of the Indian National Congress; and the first British Indian Member of Parliament. The book, published in 1901, carries, among other things, a first (and brilliant) attempt at defining a poverty line for India, and seeks an explanation of the poverty of the country in the continuous and oppressive draining of its wealth, achieved by 'plunder, not trade,' that is, through punitive taxation unredeemed by British exports into India. It is worth noting that Naoroji had anticipated Sen's 'entitlement theory' of famines, as borne out by this record of a speech addressed by him in Kennington, London, in 1900:

> It might be asked were not the famines due to droughts? His answer was in the negative. India was able to grow any quantity of food. Her resources in that respect were inexhaustible, and when famines had occurred in the past before she was subjected to the continual drain of her wealth the population were able to withstand them because they had stores of grain upon which they could fall back. But nowadays they were unable to accumulate such stores. Immediately the grain was grown it had to be sold in order to provide the taxation of the country, and the people were therefore not in a position to cope with famine. . . . [T]he difficulty of India was that the Natives had no money with which to buy food should their crops fail, and hence it was that these disastrous famines arose.

The remedy for this state of affairs was couched in equally uncompromising terms, in an address to the Plumstead Radical Club in London, in 1900:

> Considering that Britain has appropriated thousands of millions of India's wealth for building up and maintaining her British Indian Empire, and for directly drawing vast wealth to herself; that she is continuing to drain about 30,000,000 of India's wealth every year unceasingly in a variety of ways; and that she has thereby reduced the bulk of the Indian population to extreme poverty, destitution, and degradation; it is therefore her bounden duty in common justice and humanity to pay from her own exchequer the costs of all famines and diseases caused by such impoverishment.

Against the passion and rigour and intelligence of Swift and Naoroji must be set the standards to which we have sunk today, as captured in an Indian State Minister's obsession with selfies in a time of drought. The kindest explanation for such behaviour—even if it means risking sedition—is in terms of irredeemable idiocy.

Note

1 This piece was originally written in April 2016.

4 An economist's descent into crime

Notes for the reader

It is not a bad idea, every once in a while, to take a break from 'serious' economics, and to deal with peripheral issues which are associations or derivatives of the subject that constitutes its usual concerns. The present offering is a detour undertaken in this spirit of a bit of a ramble off the beaten track. It looks at how and why – apart from natural inclination – economists might take an interest in crime (or at least crime fiction).

The profit motive: fiction and the economics of crime

There are economists who take the principles of mainstream economics so seriously that they seek to explain all sorts of human phenomena in terms entirely of these principles. Proponents of what in economics is called 'Human Capital Theory' are particularly adept at this. A leading example is Gary Becker, who was awarded a Nobel Prize for Economics, and wrote on the 'economics of crime.' Not to be outdone, other practitioners have since written on, among other things, the economics of punishment, the economics of suicide, and even the economics of extra-marital affairs. This surfeit eventually drew the exasperated attention of a Princeton economist, Alan Blinder, who wrote a parody of the genre titled 'The Economics of Brushing Teeth.' Blinder's effort seems to have had little in the way of a dampening effect on the enthusiasm of the Human Capital School, which continues to turn out tracts on the economics of this and the economics of that, when it is not busy with the economics of something else.

At the heart of human motivation as it is perceived by mainstream economics is 'the profit motive'—the desire to maximize utility. Crime fiction is an excellent site for an exploration of this impulse which guides the textbook economist's understanding of human behaviour. If one comes right down to it, *homo economicus* is best regarded in the light of a machine that is designed to accumulate as much wealth as it possibly can, under the influence of two powerful driving forces, which Frank Hahn, a famous economic theorist, called 'private greed and private rationality.' Interestingly, a great deal of crime fiction is concerned with precisely this aspect of human behaviour.

Since I am both an economist and a crime fiction aficionado, I thought it might be fun to review a few of the many, many colourable ways of making profit which crime fiction has to offer, and from which the Human Capital theorist might benefit. Let me share some of my casual findings with the reader, who I hope will find it amusing to track down some of these stories if s/he is not already familiar with them. (I am concerned only with crime as it relates to money-making, and not to other motives, such as revenge, self-defence, or passion.)

It makes sense, I suppose, to begin with the Master, Sir Arthur Conan Doyle. It is amazing how many crooked ways of making money are explored in the Sherlock Holmes stories. *Blackmail* is covered in the story 'Charles Augustus Milverton' (in which Holmes and Watson themselves break the law in getting after a ruthless blackmailer). *Counterfeiting* (apparently a fairly popular crime in Victorian England) receives attention in two stories, 'The Engineer's Thumb' and 'The Three Garridebs.' *Beggary* is the subject of what Watson loved to call an example of 'the bizarre and the *outré*,' in the remarkable tale titled 'The Man with the Twisted Lip.'

Impersonation is addressed in at least two stories, and in two different ways: 'The Case of Identity' is a sadly comical story, while 'The Stockbroker's Clerk' is a grimmer account of violence. *Murder for inheritance* is a popular theme in crime fiction, and receives perhaps its most classically 'atmospheric' treatment in that extraordinary novel *The Hound of the Baskervilles*, closely paralleled by the horror of 'The Speckled Band.' (Agatha Christie's 'Wireless' is another absolutely ingenious little story in this genre.) *Betting and gambling* are at the heart of the crime committed in 'Silver Blaze,' that famous story in which mention is made of 'the curious incident of the dog in the night time.' *The Sign of Four*, like Wilkie Collins' earlier Victorian thriller *The Moonstone*, is constructed around a tale of *jewel-thievery*. G. K. Chesteron's Father Brown stories, 'The Blue Cross' and 'The Flying Stars,' are also about a gifted jewel thief, Flambeau, whom the Reverend eventually deflects to the path of virtue.

A good deal of crime is also treated lightly or comically in fiction. *Burglary*, for instance, is the theme of the 'Raffles' stories written by E. W. Hornung. Hornung was, as it happens, Conan Doyle's brother-in-law; and while Holmes and Watson were partners in detection, Raffles and Bunny were partners in crime. Raffles established the tradition of the 'gentleman burglar': his virtue was vouchsafed by the fact that when he wasn't burgling houses he was a respectable cricketer! The type of the sophisticated gentleman-crook was carried forward by Leslie Charteris' 'Saint' character Simon Templar; and John Creasy's 'Toff,' although a sleuth, was given to employing unorthodox (strictly illegal) methods of investigation.

Perhaps the most endearingly loveable criminal of fiction is the perpetually impecunious, perpetually optimistic, perpetually innovative, and perpetually unsuccessful confidence man created by P. G. Wodehouse: Stanley Featherstonehaugh (pronounced 'Fanshaw') Ukridge. A man with a limitless penchant for devising money-making schemes of the greatest ingenuity and convolution, he systematically and unwaveringly fails in every one of his plans, only to rise from the ashes of his failure in order to tackle the next scheme. This next scheme could be pinching dogs from an unfriendly aunt to conduct a 'Dog College,' or running an accident syndicate to cash in on insurance from a deliberately self-inflicted injury. The latter is an instance of what in the literature on insurance (or more broadly the literature on the economics of information) is called the 'problem of moral hazard.' Indeed, Wodehouse's fiction is instructive, in other ways too, for a student of economic theory. For example, what is fashionably called 'incentive compatibility' in the economics literature of 'implementation' is neatly summed up by an odious character of Wodehouse's—the private investigator Percy Frobisher Pilbeam—who is frequently given to asking this question before he involves himself in any activity: 'What is there in it for me?'

Kidnapping and ransom constitute another theme for the making of money in fiction. This potentially grim crime is a subject of great fun in Wodehouse's novel *The Little Nugget*, and is explored again in the novel *Laughing Gas*. A small boy kidnapped by thugs is the central character in both stories. These stories actually have a distinguished predecessor: credit for the originality of the theme informing this genre belongs elsewhere. Surely the most hilarious account of the subject has been written by O. Henry in his story 'The Ransom of Red Chief' which carries that characteristic O. Henry twist in the tail—the unexpected, and often stunning, surprise in store for the reader at the end of the story. What happens in this particular instance is—but no, let me not spoil things for the reader who hasn't yet encountered the tale. . . .

The attractions of the 'Locked-Room Mystery'

Why would a retired economist like me be interested in some sub-genre of crime fiction? Well, some economists are 'theorists,' and some theorists work on a branch of the science called 'Social Choice Theory,' which is a body of thought that lies at the intersection of economics, politics, and philosophy. Social Choice Theory is concerned with the problem of deriving meaningful procedures for the aggregation of individual preferences over

24 *On economics and economic themes*

alternative states of affairs into a collective or 'social' preference. 'Majority voting' is an example of such an aggregation mechanism, and is a subject to which early contributions were made, in the 19th century, by an Oxford University lecturer of logic and mathematics called Charles Lutwidge Dodgson, more familiarly known by his pen-name Lewis Carroll. The architect of modern Social Choice Theory is Kenneth Arrow, an economist from Stanford University and a Nobel Laureate. Arrow was interested in characterizing the class of preference aggregation mechanisms which would satisfy some innocuous properties, such as allowing for diversity of individual preferences, respecting unanimity of preferences, and disallowing dictatorship. His mathematical reasoning led Arrow to a stunning result—namely that there exists *no* preference aggregation procedure (including majority voting) that satisfies the set of seemingly reasonable properties he demanded of the aggregation mechanism. The Arrow result is a celebrated example of an 'Impossibility Theorem,' a species of reasoning in mathematical logic which suggests that a combination of individually appealing axioms that might be expected to result in a plausible and constructive proposition actually ends up, most counter-intuitively, delivering a logical impossibility. (Perhaps the most celebrated such result in the history of mathematics is due to the great mathematician Kurt Gödel, the author of 'Gödel's Result' 'on formally undecidable propositions of *Principia Mathematica* and Related Systems.')

What does any of this have to do with crime fiction? Well, in a sense, the mystery story does the *opposite* of what an Impossibility Theorem does: the latter suggests that a combination of plausible circumstances can sometimes shockingly yield an impossible outcome, while the former (when it is well crafted) suggests a combination of virtually impossible circumstances under which not just a possible, but a shockingly very real, crime is revealed to have been committed. Both varieties of intellectual exercise challenge the logical faculty of the analyst, and can—given a certain mentality which some economists share with crime-story aficionados—be a source of great fun. The Locked-Room Mystery is a specific example of the possible crime derived from impossible circumstances—in this particular case, a crime (usually murder) committed in a sealed room without apparent egress into or exit from it, or within a confined space containing a finite number of persons which is subjected to continuous monitoring of who comes in and who goes out. Restricting myself only to the short story format, let me mention six of my personal Locked-Room Mystery favourites.

In chronological order of publication, at the top of the list I should place Arthur Conan Doyle's 'The Speckled Band,' first published in 1892 in the *Strand Magazine*. Sherlock Holmes, in this story, investigates the sudden and inexplicable death of a young lady in a room locked from the inside and equipped with windows that are barred and shuttered from human passage. In the process, he prevents a second possible murder, by unraveling a scheme of deadly evil and horror.

A second outstanding story is G. K. Chesterton's 'The Secret Garden,' published in 1910 in the collection *The Innocence of Father Brown*. The atmospherics in the story—of brooding menace, of palpable evil, of monstrous intimations of grotesqueries—are virtually unrivalled in the annals of crime fiction. The discovery of a decapitated corpse in the garden of a house in which guests have assembled for a party is followed by this meekly uttered observation of the detective-priest Father Brown: 'I say, there are no gates to this garden, do you know.'

In 1914 there appeared what seems to be a little-known story called 'Death in the Excelsior.' It relates the strange case of a man found suddenly dead in the locked room of an English boarding house called 'The Excelsior.' It turns out that the cause of death is murder by poisoning. The author of the story is a most unlikely one—although he loved detective fiction, was a personal friend and admirer of Conan Doyle's (with whom he sometimes turned out to play cricket), and wrote occasional parodies of crime stories, including a delectable spoof on Sherlock Holmes in a 1903 issue of *Punch*. You can find the story on the web in the Gutenberg e-book *Death in the Excelsior and Other Stories*. The author? P. G. Wodehouse!

In 1933, 'Sapper,' the creator of Bulldog Drummond (a progenitor of Ian Fleming's James Bond), brought out a collection of mystery stories titled *Ronald Standish*, featuring the eponymous amateur detective. My Hodder and Stoughton edition proclaims the author to be 'the "inimitable" Sapper.' 'Inimitable,' perhaps, but apparently not 'non-imitating': at least three of the stories in the collection draw fairly liberally on corresponding tales in the Sherlock Holmes canon! Notwithstanding, the collection has an engaging locked-room story in it called 'The Mystery of the Slip-Coach,' in which a corpse with a bullet through the head is found in the compartment of a train. The compartment, with both door and window shut, is in a 'slip-coach' that has no connecting corridor linking with the rest of the train. The solution of the murder turns on the remains of a raw egg found in the compartment.

Two acknowledged masters of the Locked-Room Mystery are John Dickson Carr (an American) and Edmund Crispin (an Englishman). The latter wrote a series of crime novels and short stories featuring, as his detective, an Oxford don of English literature, Gervase Fen. One of these stories—'The Hunchback Cat'—is a tiny and startlingly diabolical Locked-Room Mystery involving death by a slit throat and aided, in its solution, by the presence of a tortoise-shell cat at the scene of the crime. The story was originally

26 *On economics and economic themes*

published, in 1954, in the pages of a newspaper—the London *Evening Standard*. Those, to coin a phrase, were the days!

Dickson Carr collaborated with Conan Doyle's son Adrian on a collection of stories—*The Exploits of Sherlock Holmes*, published in 1954—based on the many tantalizing references made to various of Holmes' cases in the original canon. One of these stories (written almost entirely by Doyle, *fils*) is titled 'The Adventure of the Sealed Room,' and deals with the suspected madness of a Colonel Warburton. It transpires, however, that the Colonel is a victim not so much of madness as of murder, which happens in a sealed room. The solution of the crime, it turns out, depends on how one would wield one's cutlery in order to consume oysters. Intrigued? Then read the story!

And read the other stories too, if you haven't already read them. It should keep you out of mischief, and, with luck, save you from being arrested for sedition by our zealous government.

Part II
On some tendencies in the dismal science

5 Economics
The view from above

Notes for the reader

'Toothcomber' is intellectually descended from 'Beachcomber', which was the pen-name of the English columnist J. B. Morton who wrote the *The Daily Express's* 'By the Way Column' from 1924 to 1975. The present vignettes have has been stimulated partly by the kindly thought that proper economics writing deserves a regular dose of solid economics in it, and partly by the realization that even if one were to deliberately set about doing a J. B. Morton on Economics, it might prove hard to come up with anything that could quite parallel some of the stuff that professionals in the field have been systematically dishing out – as mimicked in various minuscule pieces which Morton wrote on the subject. The presiding spirit of the pieces in this Chapter is the philosopher Harry Frankfurt's book *On Bullshit*.

By 'Toothcomber'
(A Set of Occasional Columns in *The Economic and Political Weekly*)

Inflation in an open economy

This Note is intended to be of help to the millions of ordinary unlearned people who are wondering, in a battered sort of way, about the reasons for the sustained rise in the price of onions which we are now witnessing. A first step toward uncovering causation resides in considering the specifics of a closed, compact, convex, continuum economy in an epsilon environment characterized by almost-perfect autarky. A fuller picture is yielded by opening up the economy to world trade at border-prices, in which exchange at the margin is mediated by myopic discount rates. A good part of the burden of explanation would have to be borne by the operation of incomplete Arrow-Debreu contingent markets in an economy subjected to monetary sterilization in the presence of debt-capitalization; a steep and unprecedented increase in the repo

30 *On some tendencies in the dismal science*

rate; a failure to ensure anything more than partial convertibility on the capital account; insider trading on outward bills of lading; and quasi-transitive rationality on the part of agents experiencing animal spirits inspired by methylated spirits. Add to this the super-neutrality of money, most saliently when the precautionary motive of hedging against the risks of unanticipated random walks dominates, and the impulse toward spiraling prices becomes self-sustaining. The matter is only aided by self-fulfilling conjectures in an environment of fully rational expectations buttressed by excess demand IS and LM functions fulfilling stochastic Granger-causality. While it would be beyond the scope of this brief expository piece to present anything like a closed and comprehensive model, it should not be hard to visualize that if once the appropriate Jacobeans, Hessians, Hamiltonians, Lagrangians, and Eulers have been constructed and solved for, iteratively and sequentially, the outcome of positive second-order partials in the price variable should drop automatically out of the model. Ergo, the steep rise in onion prices.

Music and economics

For all those who have wondered ceaselessly about non-sampling errors, regional variations, and the factors determining the choice of *ragas* in Carnatic music performances, it may come as edifying instruction to learn of the deep underlying connection between these phenomena on the one hand and, on the other, the economics of maximizing output dictated by a Cobb-Douglas production process. The links become apparent if we were to consider an application of Spilrajn's theorem to the transitive closure of the *Komal Rishabh* accents in *Mohana Kalyani* performed in *mishra-chaapu taalam*. The *gamakaas* of the *raga* can be legitimately modelled in terms of a two-step sequential system of equations conforming to the harmonics of a Ramsey-Euler problem in the calculus of variations, as reflected in the monotonic scalar transformation of the closely allied, but delicately differentiated, polyphonic motets of Lassus, frequently credited—yes!—to Sherlock Holmes. Of course, to go the full distance would require us to uncover the intimately paired bi-conditional implications of *Shuddha Gandhar* and *Madhyamavati*, and *Komal Dhaivat* and *Sankarabharanam*. A natural analogue to consider in this context would be the Kalai-Smorodinsky solution to the pure bargaining problem postulated by Nash, in terms of which the wholly plausible outcome of a clashing *abaswaram* is subtly deflected to a fully determinate, unique, and stable equilibrium. By contrast, by examining the co-evolution of *Prati Madhyama* in *Pantuvarali* and *Kaisiki Nishada* in *Reetigowla*, we are enabled to recover the original, canonical Nash solution and—in a dynamic context—the sub-game perfect equilibrium of Selten and Harsyani. For a dissenting note on this, the reader is advised to follow the closely-reasoned analytics of the optimal solution to an infinite-horizon inter-temporal planning problem in the economics literature and the startlingly parallel treatment of *manodharmic kalpanaswaras* and their resolution, via *shrutilaya*, in Carnatic music.

Why the poor are profligate

Some of the most foundational questions confronting our economy and society are typically viewed through the distorting prism of ideology, and dealt with with that mix of 'radical' *force majeure* and hot-headed rhetorical flourish that so thoroughly characterizes a good deal of allegedly 'professional' opinion in such matters, and so disastrously negates the advantages that are to be had from a dispassionate application of the tools of formal economic analysis to real-life problems. This is nowhere more plainly in evidence than in addressing such phenomena as deprivation and disparity. Take the case of the profound failure of the poor in our economy to contribute even marginally to the growth process because of their unwillingness to save. A standard response to this crippling drag on the economy is constituted by the surly, radical view that the poor can scarcely be expected to save when they do not even have enough to consume. There may be some cheap popularity to be gained from such apparently public-spirited ripostes in behalf of the unwashed millions, but, really, such ill-manneredness is in the end a reflection of little more than wholesale ignorance of how much it would benefit the poor in particular, and the economy at large, to equip the deprived sections of society with a quasi-linear utility function. Even a passing familiarity with Banach spaces and a fairly standard application of functional analysis to an optimum savings problem which is mediated by constrained maximization of a quasi-linear or hyper-geometric utility function should convince one of the paramount urgency of leaving it to rational expectations within the context of an unregulated market to engender the saving habit in the poor through the purely evolutionarily strategic dominance that the spontaneous dynamic assimilation of logarithmic convexity of the (appropriately compact) preference set might be expected to achieve. Of course, we are here speaking only of sufficient conditions. A proper characterization theorem would be beyond the scope of this brief column, and it would be pointless to attempt anything of that nature here. However, a few pointers in the desired direction may not come amiss. The Convex Utility Function (CUF) Theorem is completely derived in a paper of mine which draws extensively on Kleene's *Meta-Mathematics*, and is substantially assisted by drawing even more extensively on Old Monk rum. (I could tell you things about the latter when combined with lemon juice, but the Editor will not have it.)

32 On some tendencies in the dismal science

Understanding inequality

There is a rumour abroad that economic inequality has been on the rise. At the heart of the rumour is casual, if not outright cavalier, empiricism, compounded by the impulses to which popular radicalism is naturally prey. The outcome is the periodic outbreak of uncouth demonstrations in locales as far-flung as Zuccotti Park in the U.S. and the streets of Brasilia in Brazil. Speaking of uncouthness, one is led, by a natural association of ideas, to journals such as the *Economic and Political Weekly* (presided over by that sinister Editor with the goatee), which have systematically served as a platform for the canard, put out by untrained economists who have never headed an Expert Committee nor estimated a regression equation in loglinear form, that growth in India has been non-inclusive. The heroic voices that have sought to resist this slander have been generally ignored. To these voices, for what it is worth, I now add mine. Posterity will judge the issue.

It is a matter, in the end, of getting the protocols of measurement right. Where ignorance is bliss, it is a simple matter to turn one's back on the requirements of scale invariance in an inequality measure which, itself, is simply a mapping from the non-negative orthant of n-dimensional Euclidean space to the non-negative real line. (I take it, of course, that inequality is amenable to real-valued representation. I desist here, in the interests of simplicity and easy exposition, from treating inequality judgements as being susceptible to interpretation as binary relations that are orderings, or, even less demandingly, as quasi-orders. I hope it is appreciated that I here make a genuine effort to impart complex ideas as simply as possible to scholars weak in formal logic and strong in prejudice. Not that I am against being illogical: I myself often am, but deliberately so, and not for reasons of ignorance. Thus are learning and stupidity differentiated.) Under scale invariance an inequality measure preserves value—as it should—when any n-dimensional income-vector is subjected to multiplication by a positive scalar. Anarchists may submit to intermediate real-valued measures of inequality governed by the Bossert-Pfingsten restriction, but that will not take away from the fact that the allegation of non-inclusive growth in India is no more than a piece of orchestrated false propaganda. It is born of *ressentiment*, pure and simple, and a denial of the virtues of a monotonic welfare function.

The economics of land acquisition

The recently orchestrated opposition to the Land Acquisition Bill is the final nail on the lid of the coffin of Development. The last fig-leaf hitherto employed to cover the nakedness of the radical view of development has now been shed. A new watermark, which plumbs the depths of shamelessness of the anti-development brigade, has been established. The Government serves an ace, and the Opposition hits it for six. Sophisticated anchors on TV programmes, who bat for the Bill and challenge its critics with sarcastic questions, are actually answered by the critics with a brazenly unanswerable logic that displays no respect for the anchors' Oxbridge accents. The critics even go so far as to suggest that the anchors must allow them time to answer their questions. What is this, if not the invasion of the body-snatchers? I am strongly tempted to ask: 'Whither India?,' or, even (after the manner of letter-writers in South Indian dailies): '*Quo vadis?*.' It reduces my anguish to pause and admire my own prose, but only a little: the concerted attack on the Bill goes deep and cuts me to the quick. For how and when can these philistines be made to understand that the stubborn resistance of a few (or several) inconsequential agents with an irrational attachment to their pieces of land cannot be allowed to come in the way of the larger good? That industry must prosper and India must grow? That, as the great utilitarian Jeremy Bentham put it, 'Natural rights is simple nonsense; natural and imprescriptible rights . . . [is] rhetorical nonsense, nonsense upon stilts'? That bleeding hearts must not be permitted to arrest the evolution of one's country into a super-power? Forgive me if my passion causes me to mix my metaphors, but surely my meaning must be clear. If it is not, all you have to do, in the cause of complete clarity, is to appeal to the Coase Theorem. Or acquaint yourself with the law-and-economics literature on liability rules, concentrating on the work of scholars who uphold the primacy of efficiency, while assiduously ignoring the work of upstarts who will insist on a view of justice that transcends considerations of Pareto optimality and so will muddy the water with talk of human rights and the like. A couple of quick theorems on the efficiency of exchange economies with and without convexity should do the job. The barbarians must be beaten back.

Cricket as a game

Fellows like Neville Cardus, with their purple prose and sentimental descriptions, have succeeded in obscuring the fact that cricket, in the end, is a game. It is all very well to suggest, as Cardus does, when speaking of Ranjitsinhji in that book *The Summer Game*, that '[o]ne after another the procession increases as it moves across our sunset stage . . . ; but all of them, no matter how high they stood, overshadowed at last by the most wonderful batsman of the lot, inexplicable unless in terms of genius.' Where is there in any of this the suggestion that cricket is a game? That

34 *On some tendencies in the dismal science*

it can be described in terms of sets of players, of n-tuples of strategies, of payoff functions, and of solution concepts? Of implementability and incentive compatibility? As in other areas of human endeavour and human knowledge, the savages have taken charge. They will speak of Bradman and Compton in terms that have no space for Nash equilibria, or the lack thereof. In the 1948 England-Australia Test series, Compton resorted to lofting the ball over the fielders' heads when Bradman brought the field in, and tapping the ball for singles when Bradman spread the field. Bradman is reported to have complained that this wasn't cricket. A more lettered man would have remarked on the non-existence of a Nash Equilibrium. The matter becomes altogether worse when discussion turns to such phenomena as spot-fixing and betting. Commentators tend to lose themselves in turgidities of moral disapprobation when what they ought to be doing is devising optimal betting strategies that take due note of random walks, conditional probabilities, rational expectations, and Bayesian priors. It is the same lack of clinical scientific analysis which bedevils much of the radical community's appreciation of our economic problems and how these ought to be addressed by the guardians of the economics profession: the failure to see that the whole thing is essentially a game. Economics professionals, like all other agents in an economy, are, after all, players. Why should only they, and bureaucrats, and politicians, be expected to behave irrationally? Where is the justice (and this is addressed to all those who are chronically and tiresomely given to bleating on the subject)—where is the justice, I ask, of denying a fellow such as myself the right to maximize my utility function when everybody else is maximizing his (or hers, in the interests of gender-sensitivity)?

Subsidies

It is very hard for the theorist to make his voice heard above the raucous din of the uncultured voices that emanate from the underworld of a gaggle of radical elements who systematically inhabit the pages of such print excrescences as the *Economic and Political Weekly*, in which they make their case, once every seven days, for populist schemes, unproductive freebies, and other exchequer-bankrupting doles and handouts to the unwashed millions. The beast must be bearded in its own den, which is the death-defying reason for the present column. To see why subsidies are economically unviable, shall we give the voice of reason a brief chance to express itself? Imagine an economy in which preferences are represented by a suitably transformed Lebesgue integral, while technology is encompassed in a connected and convex Haufsdorf space that

Economics 35

is interrupted (almost everywhere) by rapidly converging sequences of complex irrationals defined on the imaginary metric of a latticed manifold. The Lie fields of the corresponding sigma-algebra will of course be assumed to be amenable to convex representation on the coordinates of the relevant saddle-point. The inter-temporal budget constraint is obtained by bond- or tax-financed income streams discounted over an infinite horizon. The optimal solution is derived from application of an extended turnpike theorem. In non-technical terms, the solution suggests that the only possible stationary stable states with subsidies are those characterized by bankruptcy and irredeemable debt over-hangs. The empirical evidence for the proposition, based on cross-country regressions, is summarized in the accompanying figure. It is too much to hope, of course, that any of this will make the least difference to the clamours from Babel for free food, schools, healthcare, and internet. Before you know it, they will be yelling for free underwear. The barbarians are at the gates.

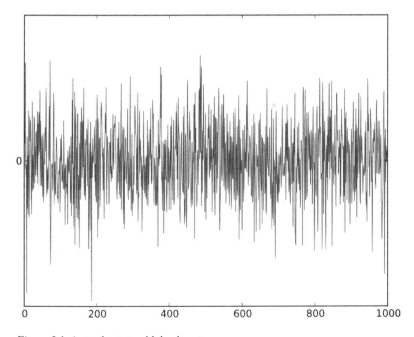

Figure 5.1 A steady state with bankruptcy

Source: https://commons.wikimedia.org/wiki/Category:White_noise#/media/File:White_noise.svg

Taxes

You cannot have subsidies if you do not have taxes: this is the inexorable logic which the rabble employs in order to ensure the inevitability of both death and taxation, the one by the other. So grab the hapless capitalist and soak the blighter in deluges of wealth, estate, gift, sales, value-added, excise, and customs taxes. Strangle incentives, crush enterprise, and retard growth in the cause of the human right of the non-labouring poor to track the IPL scores on their free laptops when they are not checking out on Katrina Kaif. Alternatively, consider a simple dynamic model of optimal incentives in a smooth, convex exchange economy characterized by asymmetric information amongst agents producing and consuming competitively in an overlapping generations model. Each agent is assumed to live two periods. In period 1, it works, produces, and procreates; in period 2, it consumes off its savings from period 1, bequeaths wealth to its offspring born in period 1 (and grown to adulthood now in period 2), and dies. What is the optimal

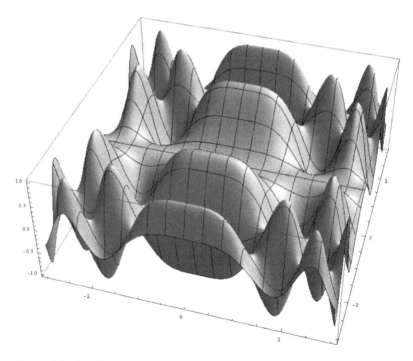

Figure 5.2 The effect on the poor of taxing the rich

Source: Solid Geometry Figure from https://commons.wikimedia.org/wiki/File:Three-dimensional_graph.png

inter-temporal saving rate? In the absence of taxation, we are assured of a strict interior solution, one which fully respects the Kuhn-Tucker conditions, converges in a finite number of generations on a steady-state stable equilibrium, and keeps the poor from frittering away their time on cricket and film-stars. But allow for distortionary taxation in the model—and all hell breaks loose: a corner solution compatible with zero or even negative savings rates and degenerate growth. The short-run evidence is all that the rabble cares for. This evidence, based on cross-country regressions, is presented in the figure, which features the effects of multidimensionally distorting taxes on the welfare of the tax-beneficiary (observe the smugness on the beneficiary's countenance).

The economics of incentives

Elected governments are under constant pressure to rush headlong into the catastrophe of public bankruptcy. The agents of this pressure are economists tutored only in the more ersatz aspects of what these rousers of the rabble are pleased to call 'political economy.' Economic incentives are nowhere more imperiled than by the widely-prevalent state practice of committing honest tax-payers' incomes to such monumental follies as public works programmes, public distribution systems, and producers' and consumers' subsidies doled out in the name of 'food security.' Even casual acquaintance with the economics of information would deflect such dangerously adventurist policies from the inevitable evils of adverse selection and moral hazard. It is arrogance toward the basic principles of targeting that pre-empts rational thought on the subject, and promotes uncouth and bellicose demands for 'universalism' in the provisioning of public benefits. For what, really, is at the heart of successful implementation? It is the recognition of the paramountcy of ensuring that the outcome of collective choice, suitably constrained by the requirements of monotonicity, neutrality, and anonymity, should respect the Revelation Principle, by lying in the core of the voting game. The 'soft' core is necessary, while the 'hard' core is sufficient. Characterization of the necessary *and* sufficient conditions for incentive-compatibility is an open problem, but one within reach of a solution. Pending that, there is surely enough theoretical evidence that has been garnered, in a variety of environments ranging from cooperative games with coalition-proof Nash equilibria to noncooperative games with subgame perfect Selten-Harsyani equilibria, to uphold the veracity of the following empirical propositions on incentives. Doling out jobs or food or medical care to the poor promotes only the incentives for sloth and brigandry. On the other hand, subsidies for export promotion, land-transfers from unproductive marginal cultivators

38 *On some tendencies in the dismal science*

to growth-oriented industrialists, systematic reductions in marginal rates of direct income taxation, and exemption of taxes on wealth, estate and corporate profit—all of these are instances of genuine economic incentives designed to ensure the implementation of efficient economic outcomes that are proof against the temptations of unilateral defection. But this, to coin a phrase, is a cry in the wilderness. Where common sense and formal analysis are abused in favour of motivated sloganeering, it is simply a matter of the mob having already gathered in order to storm the Bastille of rational thought and orderly progress. The louts, even as I write, are sharpening their knives.

The imperium of economics

It is amazing, and impressive, to contemplate the dominion held by the discipline of economics over human affairs, to meditate the breadth and richness of human experience it has succeeded in explaining, and all of this with the aid of such parsimonious assumptions on the wellsprings of human motivation as it has summoned to its aid—extending, in their splendid and narrow austerity, to just two axioms which the economist Frank Hahn has called the axioms of 'private greed and private rationality.' Armed with no more than an increasing and strictly concave utility function (which is at least twice continuously differentiable), we have nailed an ever-increasing range of economic, social, and psychological behaviours, as reflected in the definitive accounts we have of the Economics of Crime, the Economics of Punishment, the Economics of Education, the Economics of Marriage, the Economics of Childbearing, the Economics of Bequests, the Economics of the Rotten Kid, the Economics of Homicide, the Economics of Suicide, the Economics of Divorce, and the Economics of Extra-Marital Affairs. (I leave out of the list an absurd effort at parody made by a discontented member of the profession, last heard of from Princeton University in the U.S.A., when he published a tract under the title of The Economics of Brushing Teeth, and justified the employment of dummy variables in his estimating equation on the true but offensive ground that his was a paper in the Human Capital framework.) In our own environment we would do well to undertake systematic studies on the Economics of Extortion, the Economics of Bribery, the Economics of Banning, the Economics of Defence Deals, the Economics of Nice Child Labour, the Economics of Cozy Capitalism, the Economics of Theocratic Governance, the Economics of Promoting the Virtues Of Tobacco, the Economics of Suppressing Dissent, the Economics of Match-Fixing, etc. We should feel free to employ as many

Economics 39

dummies as we please—1.3 billion sounds like a nice number. Here is a helpful visual aid to understanding the Economics of Everything, based on nothing more than the aforementioned assumptions of private greed and private rationality:

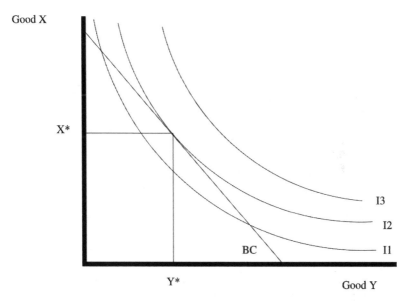

Figure 5.3 Bliss

Source: https://commons.wikimedia.org/wiki/File:Consumer_constraint_choice.svg

6 Hyman Kaplan and the G*L*O*B*A*L P*O*V*E*R*T*Y L*I*N*E

Notes for the reader

This essay is premised on the notion that policy-makers and involved lay readers are entitled to have an insight into how global money-metric poverty statistics are presently (unreasonably) conceptualized – and how they might be (more reasonably) formulated. This is a matter of such direct, if foundational, global justice that it deserves a widespread and inclusive understanding of the issues involved. Accordingly, the essay is aimed at presenting an expository account of the World Bank's methodology of assessing country-specific and global income-poverty. The methodology, in the author's view, is logically flawed, apart from being politically conservative. The present essay has been written, with a view to stimulating the widest possible popular interest, in the style of one of Leo Rosten's well-known H*y*m*a*n K*a*p*l*a*n stories.

It had all begun innocuously enough, reflected Mr Parkhill ruefully, as he looked back on the events of the evening. It occurred to him that it was a cardinal feature of Beginners' Grade that things *always* began innocuously enough there, before they metamorphosed fantastically into those monstrous and outrageous affairs which his temple of learning was increasingly becoming a site of. Sentence construction, Mr Parkhill admonished himself severely. He also took himself to task for ending a sentence with a preposition, a vileness which one ought, he believed, to perpetrate no more in thought than in speech. Switching the focus of his disapprobation from himself to his fate, why, he asked his immortal soul tiredly, did he always end up presiding over these anarchic situations? Need he have asked? The self-evident answer flashed across his mind's eye in glorious Technicolor, the red letters shadowed in blue and separated, lovingly, one from the other, in stars of emerald green: H*Y*M*A*N K*A*P*L*A*N.

The Class had been untypically lacking in energy that evening, and in an innocent bid to hello-jolly them into a state of something approximating wakefulness, he had exhorted his flock in these terms: "Come, Class, a little show of engagement, if you please! Learning the *lingua franca* is an indispensable key to leading the good life, so may I ask for a little more effort all round?"

This had been the unwitting trigger to Apocalypse.

"The good lives, the *best* lives," moaned Olga Tarnova of the husky throat, "are Rossian, all Rossian."

"Is Chris Columbus no good then?" enquired Mr Pinsky with elaborate sarcasm, the while slapping his cheek.

"Likevise Alexander the Great? Or perhaps it is Alexander the Stoopid?" Thus Mr Reubens Olansky.

"Oy!" grunted Mrs Moskowitz, which could be interpreted as a comment signalling even-handededly bipartisan criticism.

"And Greta Garbo?" queried timid Miss Mitnick anxiously.

Miss Tarnova waved the barbarians' questions away with a languid and bejewelled hand. "The good lives, the best lives," she repeated throatily, "are all Rossian. Tchaikovsky, Rimsky-Korsakov, Tolstoy, Dostoevsky, Nureyev, Pavlova—"

"And you hevvink no room for even vun non-Rossian in your list of the good lives, Tarnova?" The question, uttered softly and suavely, and pregnant with silken menace and the promise of a fatal hidden trap, emanated from the lips of Hyman Kaplan.

"Esk her," encouraged loyal Pinsky, slapping his cheek again.

"Answer yourself," commanded Olga Tarnova, with regal contempt. "Vun name, that is all I ask, just vun name from outside Rossia that is more great than Tchaikovsky or Rimsky-Korsakov or Tolstoy."

"Perheps you hev never come across this name?" wafted in tones even silkier from her adversary. "Perheps the Star of Beginnis' Grate is unknown to you? Perheps, Tarnova, you hev not had the pleasure, plizz, of ever knowing the name of—Hymie Keplen?"

Mr Kaplan, an *agent provocateur* to beat all *agents provocateurs*, had outdone himself on this occasion. The reactions followed quick and fast.

"Pffft!" said Mr Pinsky admiringly.

"Holy Smoky!" said Mr Stanislaus Wilkomirski.

"God forgive such prodness!" said Mr Peter Studniczka, a sexton in real life.

"*Pride*, Mr Studniczka, *pride*," corrected Mr Parkhill, skilfully diagnosing the sexton's intended rendering of the abstract noun form of 'proud.'

Gentle Miss Mitnick was devastated. Barely managing to keep the tears out of her voice, she wished to know how "Mr Kaplan is standing himself besite Dostoevsky, Columbus, and Greta Garbo?"

"Perheps Keplen is more beautiful than Garbo. Perheps he hev more shapeful legs," hooted Mr Nathan P. Nathan.

Bereft of rational explanation, Olga Tarnova was inclined to lay Mr Kaplan's hubris at the door of insanity rather than villainy. "Mod!" she moaned. "Mod! Mod!"

This was beginning to get out of hand. Mr Parkhill moved in swiftly and firmly. "Class," he said, "My reference to 'the good life' was not intended to move you to a—er—parochial appropriation, to your own respective nationalities, of all the great lives lived upon earth. By 'the good life,' I had in mind," continued Mr Parkhill, rather allowing himself to be carried away a little, "the Aristotelian notion of human flourishing, of a fulfilling material, intellectual, and—ah—spiritual life."

"Not possible," asserted Mr Kaplan vehemently, "vithout owning planty caboodle."

"If your reference is to the possession of money," said Mr Parkhill, "the relevant colloquialism is, I believe, 'boodle,' not 'caboodle,' though both terms may also be employed interchangeably to refer to an entire group, or collection, of people."

"Yes, money," said Mr Kaplan lovingly. "Vun must have money for the good life. Vithout, is life of poverty."

"True indeed," said Mr Parkhill. And then he made the fatal mistake. "How much money, do you think, does one need to avoid poverty?"

Earnest Miss Mitnick, who made a strenuous effort to keep herself *au courant* with the affairs of the world, volunteered this intelligence: "According to Vold Bank, vun dollar per day. Ektually, in 1990 it was 1.02 Purchasing Power Parity dollars in 1985 prices; in 2000, it was 1.08 PPP dollars in 1993 prices; and now, after 2008, it is 1.25 PPP dollars in 2005 prices. Commonly referred to as 'dollar-a-day' international poverty line."

"Vun dollar per day! Ha! *Ha!* What this vun dollar per day is?" said Mr Blattberg derisively.

"It is Vold Bank's Poverty Line," explained Miss Mitnick, patiently if self-referentially.

"Voild Bank is *valcome* to living on vun dollar per day," said Mr Kaplan generously. "I do not *object* to Praz'dent of Voild Bank earning 30 dollars a month. But I do object to pipple saying that Hymie Keplen is a malted millionaire if he earn more than 360 dollars a year. Oh, yes, I object. I object planty."

"*Multi*-millionaire, Mr Kaplan," corrected Mr Parkhill gently.

"But—but—" stammered poor Miss Mitnick. "Vold Bank is using scientific methods of all kinds economics and statistics to arrive at dollar-a-day poverty line."

"Perheps Keplen is great economist," said Mr Olansky subversively. "Perheps Keplen is working in spare hours on secret formula for Poverty Line which get him the Nobel Prize!"

"Mitnick, Olansky, you also most valcome to become malted millionaires on vun dollar per day. Let me not stop you."

"Pffft!" said Mr Pinsky, slapping his cheek.

The G*L*O*B*A*L P*O*V*E*R*T*Y L*I*N*E   43

"Give an *inch*, Kaplan," pleaded Miss Shimmelfarb. "In India, poverty line is even less than vun dollar per day. It is a way of speaking. Any poverty line is artiberry—"

"*Arbitrary*, Miss Shimmelfarb," said Mr Parkhill.

"Thank you, Mr Pockheel. Any poverty line is ar-bit-ra-ry this way or that," continued Miss Shimmelfarb carefully. "It is a way of speaking. But one has to have *some* poverty line to see if the number of people below the poverty line is increasing or decreasing over time. And in the voild—also in many countries like India—the number of people below the poverty line is decreasing with time. That is good think, if poverty is becoming less and less. Why you want to spoil the Voild Bank's party, Kaplan?"

"Because, Shimmelfarb, Voild Bank's party is not *mine* party. Is poverty becoming less and less if poverty line is $2.50 instead of $1.25?"

"Do you have—er—an *argument* to offer, Mr Kaplan?" enquired Mr Parkhill, who never despaired of the possibility of steering his Class toward more rational forms of discourse than their heightened emotional involvement in their various subjects of discussion often permitted.

"Is axcellent point, as alvays, from Mr Pockheel," purred Mr Kaplan approvingly. "Our tichcher is asking for *rizzon and logick*, not slep-beng remocks ottered vit'out t'inking and sanse. Kindly pay attention, Shimmelfarb, Studniczka, Olansky, Mitnick, leddies and gantlemen, fallow-members of Beginnis' Grate," continued the paragon of reason and logic. "Kindly tell me: what *minns* 'poverty line'?"

"Perhaps you will tell us, Mr Kaplan?" said Mr Parkhill, gently nudging Mr Kaplan, even as Socrates had nudged his own acolytes, from the undisciplined delights of rhetoric to the civilized pleasures of reasoning. "What *does* the expression 'poverty line' mean?"

"It minns," said Mr Kaplan, smoothing his tie, "that money, or income, is a *minns*, not an *and*."

"A means, and not an end," repeated Mr Parkhill. "A means to *what*, Mr Kaplan?"

"A minns to avoiding vant in *anodder* space, the space of 'fonctionings'."

"That is a most interesting thought, Mr Kaplan," said Mr Parkhill, impressed despite himself. "Mr Kaplan makes the reasonable point, as I see it, that a poverty line specified in income terms is—presumably by virtue of its being *called* a 'poverty line'—a means to the end of avoiding poverty in the space of 'functionings.' A 'functioning' is what the economist Professor Amartya Sen calls 'a state of being or doing'—a state of being well-nourished, for example, or mobile, or in possession of knowledge, or in reasonably good health, or able to 'appear in public without shame.' Am I correct, Mr Kaplan?"

44 *On some tendencies in the dismal science*

'You are *alvays* correct, Mr Pockheel," said Mr Kaplan, making it plain that no one who had the honour of being his, Mr Kaplan's, mentor could ever be found guilty of error.

"So what, Keplen," queried Mr Olansky, "if 'poverty line' is a minns to an and?"

"So *this*, Olansky," replied Mr Kaplan. "If 'poverty line' is a minns to the and of avoiding vant in the space of fonctionings, how come the poverty line is vun dollar for you and me and the whole kit and caboodle? If 'poverty line' is a minns to avoiding vant in the space of fonctionings, how should we fix the poverty line? Like so. For me, for you, for itch of us, we first ask: 'What is the rizzonable cost of avoiding hunger? Avoiding ignorance? Achieving mobility? Being in good health? Being a part of our community?' We then edd up all the costs, and the sum is the poverty line. But because our nidds are different, our poverty lines should be different. You and I, Olansky, have to spand money on Beginnis Grate to learn English, but not so a native Yankee. I nidd to spand money on a dantist for my kevvities, but not you, Olansky, who have strong tith from eating babies alive. I hev to spand money for my son's Bar Mitzvah, but not you, pagan Olansky. If Mitnick marries and bears child" (Miss Mitnick was observed blushing furiously), "then she nidd to spand more money on food then you, Olansky, who are alraddy obis. Mitnick nidd more money than a person in South India to keep warm in winter. A person in South India nidd more food than Mitnick, because food in South India is poorly absorbed due to amoebas in the water. So how come vun dollar per day is the *same* poverty line for itch of us? Explain me, Olansky."

Mr Olansky drew a deep breath, and Mr Parkhill exploited the opportunity to move in swiftly before Beginners' Grade was exposed to a blast of Olansky eloquence. "Mr Kaplan," explained Mr Parkhill in the best tradition of the helpful interlocutor, "offers us much food for thought. It is his contention that the language of a 'poverty line' is compatible only with a view of income as a means to an end, specifically, the means to the end of avoiding deprivation in functioning space. If this is accepted, then in view of the fact that there are both individual and context- or environment-dependent heterogeneities, making for inter-personal differences in the ability to transform incomes into functionings, the case for a unique money-metric poverty line loses much of its force. Putting it differently, it is unquestionably true that the standard in terms of which poverty is measured must be invariant across regimes if poverty comparisons are to be meaningful. But the language of the 'poverty line' strongly suggests that it is invariance of the poverty standard in the space of *functionings*, rather than of *incomes*, that must be maintained. This, indeed, is the essence of Amartya Sen's oft-repeated sentiment that poverty is best regarded as an absolute notion in the space of functionings, but—and precisely for that reason—as a relative notion in the space of real incomes (the World Bank's identification methodology ought to take note of this), or commodity bundles (the Government of India's official methodology ought to take note of this), or resources in general. We can agree, Class, can we not, that Mr Kaplan has furnished us with a cogent argument against the World Bank's dollar-a-day advocacy, and related poverty identification approaches?"

In reactions ranging from immediately delighted acquiescence to belatedly reluctant acceptance, Mr Kaplan's point of view, it became clear, gradually found favour with the denizens of Beginners' Grade. Mr Kaplan bowed modestly. He was not, however, quite done.

"If the lengwidge of 'poverty line' is used," resumed Mr Kaplan, "then we must hev at least group-specific poverty lines: *vun* poverty line for averybody in a country—not to mention the voild—is absurd, crazy, bobo, unbelievabubble, weird! No point in using bad lengwidge and then making axcuse of unavoidable artiberriness in fixing the poverty line. This is ebbuse of lengwidge, rizzon, and logick. But what if the minning of income is taken differently? What if income is seen not as a minns to an and but as an and in itself?"

"Well, then, Mr Kaplan," invited Mr Parkhill. "What if we were to—ah—abjure the language of the 'poverty line,' and interpret income in the light of an end in itself rather than as a means to the end of avoiding deprivation? Would this open up some other way of assessing money-metric poverty, one that avoids the standard identification-followed-by-aggregation procedure?"

"Yes, Mr Pockheel, it vould," averred Mr Kaplan. "I vould soggest that we should use the quintile income statistic of Professor Kaushik Basu as a poverty indicator. Very smart dude, Kaushik Basu, despite being former Chief Economic Advisor to Government of India and present Wise Praz'dent of Voild Bank. Looks like Voody Allen and is one or two times as smart. We hear that Voild Bank is planning to give systematic information on the average income of the poorest 40 per cent of each country's population. If income is seen as an and in itself, then the 'income-poor' of a country are, for example, the income-poorest 10 or 15 or 20 or 25 or 30 or 40 per cent of the population. Ornerry logick. Say 20 per cent (which make more sanse than Voild Bank's 40 per cent), and the average income of the poorest 20 per cent is the *quintile income statistic*—'Q.' In a plain and simple way, Q is an income poverty indicator, when income is taken to minn an and in itself. Q should replace Voild Bank's 'dollar-a-day' headcount estimates of poverty, which are minningless. At a point of time, countries can be compared for their income poverty in terms of their levels of Q. Over time, and for itch country, or for the voild as a whole, we can see how Q is moving. We can set targets for the growth of Q. For exemple, if the growth rate of per capita

GNP is fixed at *x* per cent per year (which is something many countries do), then we can esk: what should be the level of Q such that, say, 50 per cent of the growth in income is distributed across quintiles in the prazent proportion and 50 per cent of the growth is divided equally among the quintiles? Call this Q*. We can now compare the *ektual* Q with Q* in itch year, to see if the income-poverty indicator is keeping up with, or moving away from, its target levels. This will give a more real picture of income poverty trends than dollar-a-day headcount estimates. We can do more than this. Suppose M and M* are defined for *richest* quintile just as Q and Q* are defined for poorest quintile. We can compare the ratio of Q to Q*—call it *q*—for the poorest quintile with the ratio of M to M* for the richest quintile—call it *m*. If these ratios are vun in itch year over time, we have a case of 'inclusive growth.' If the *q*-ratios are less than vun and the *m*-ratios are greater than vun, and if the ratios are also moving away from each other over time, we have a case of growing dynomic inequality. Q is a wery wersatile index. It is a poverty indicator, an inequality indicator, and can be used to measure the 'inclusiveness' of growth. But for that, Voild Bank should use the statistic visely and vell, and not for kismetic purposes or by being too clever in halves."

"*Cosmetic* purposes, Mr Kaplan, and '*too clever by half*'," corrected Mr Parkhill. "Well, I must say that I find Mr Kaplan's advocacy of the 'quintile income statistic' as a measure of money-metric poverty *simpliciter* (as the philosopher would put it), and as a means of diagnosing inequality and the inclusiveness or otherwise of growth, to be very persuasive. We may well discover that Q suggests we live in a world of greater income-poverty and inequality than we have so far been led to believe is the case."

"Hurrah for Keplen!" hailed Mr Pinsky. "Keplen will now lead us to Zuccotti Park!"

There was no denying Hyman Kaplan now. He was, without doubt, the darling of Beginners' Grade, even amongst his most seasoned and hardbitten adversaries. As the bell tolled to signal the end of a momentous session, the Class gathered around its elected leader, slapping him on the back and congratulating him on its noisy, shuffling way out of the classroom. It was then that Mr Parkhill reviewed, rapidly, in his mind's eye, the events of the last hour, and which have formed the substance of this account.

As he came swiftly to the end of his review, his eye caught that of Mr Kaplan, who had turned at the head of the stairs and waved a deferentially fraternal hand at him. "Von't you join us, Mr Pockheel?" he asked. "It vould be an honour." "Yes!" chorused the rest of Beginners' Grade. "Please, Mr Pockheel!" Mr Parkhill hesitated for no more than a moment. "What the heck!" he said to himself, as he joined his jostling, chattering flock.

*

Three hours later, as they were being evicted from Zuccotti Park by the police, Mr Parkhill's class, under the leadership of Mr Kaplan, gave lusty expression, one more time, to the sentiment that They Were The 99 Per Cent. Mr Parkhill, his hair tousled, his clothes dishevelled, his spectacles perched all anyhow on his nose, his tie askew, and his face flushed, said modestly and *sotto voce*: "Yay!"

He had to admit it to himself. For almost the first time in his life, Mr Parkhill felt—well—l*i*b*e*r*a*t*e*d.

Further recommended reading

Basu, K. (2001). 'On the Goals of Development,' in G. M. Meier and J. E. Stiglitz (eds.), *Frontiers of Development Economics: The Future in Perspective*, Oxford University Press: New York.

Basu, K. (2006). 'Globalization, Poverty, and Inequality: What Is the Relationship? What Can Be Done?' *World Development*, 34(8): 1361–1373.

Basu, K. (2013). 'Shared Prosperity and the Mitigation of Poverty: In Practice and in Precept,' Policy Research Working Paper No. WPS 6700. The Worldbank: Washington, DC. Available at: http://documents.worldbank.org/curated/en/2013/11/18506691/shared-prosperity-mitigation-poverty-practice-precept.

Pogge, T. (2010). 'How Many Poor Should There Be? A Rejoinder to Ravallion,' in S. Anand, P. Segal and J. E. Stiglitz (eds.), *Debates on the Measurement of Global Poverty*, Oxford University Press: New York.

Ravallion, M. (2010). 'A Reply to Reddy and Pogge,' in S. Anand, P. Segal and J. E. Stiglitz (eds.), *Debates on the Measurement of Global Poverty*, Oxford University Press: New York.

Reddy, S. (2004). 'A Capability-Based Approach to Estimating Global Poverty,' *In Focus: Dollar a Day How Much Does It Say?*, United Nations Development Programme, September 6–8.

Reddy, S. and T. Pogge (2010). 'How *Not* to Count the Poor,' in S. Anand, P. Segal and J. E. Stiglitz (eds.), *Debates on the Measurement of Global Poverty*, Oxford University Press: New York. (A version is also available at: www.socialanalysis.org.)

Ross, Q. L. [Leo Rosten] (1937). *The Education of H*Y*M*A*N K*A*P*L*A*N*, Harcourt, Brace: New York.

Ross, Q. L. [Leo Rosten] (1959). *The Return of H*Y*M*A*N K*A*P*L*A*N*, Harper: New York.

Sen, A. K. (1983). 'Poor, Relatively Speaking,' *Oxford Economic Papers*, 35(2): 153–169.

Subramanian, S. (2011). '"Inclusive Development" and the Quintile Income Statistic,' *Economic and Political Weekly*, 46(4): 69–72.

Subramanian, S. (2013). 'Poverty and Inclusive Growth in the Light of the Quintile Income Stastistic,' November–December Issue of WIDER Angle (UNU-WIDER's Newletter), Helsinki. Available at: www.wider.unu.edu/publications/newsletter/articles-2013/en_GB/11-12-2013-subramanian/.

7 A Leacockian view of economics today

Notes for the reader

Stephen Leacock published a book called *Nonsense Novels* in 1911. Drawing mainly on the stories in that volume (and indeed employing the same titles), and also on some other of Leacock's writings, the ensuing offerings are a re-telling of the Leacock pieces employing themes in economics and economics-related matters. It is worth recalling that Leacock himself was an economist, being, in real life, Professor of Political Economy at McGill University, Canada. The excuse for the present set of imitations of imitations is that the author, like Leacock, was also a professor of Economics who had to retire for reasons of growing old but not (just as in Leacock's case) for reasons of growing up.

Maddened by mystery

It was on a wild and wintry evening of the year '15, I find recorded in my notebook, that the world first became acquainted with that chain of singular circumstances which led to the arrival, in the drawing room of our humble quarters, of an entity that at first sight appeared to be a drone but turned out, when once the disguise had been penetrated, to be, instead, the President of the United States of America, who found my friend swathed in a mouse-coloured dressing gown, his eyes concealed behind a pair of violet goggles, his upper lip adorned by a luxurious red false moustache, and his head wreathed in clouds of smoke from a Meerschaum filled with shag stuffed from a Persian slipper.

"Pray take a seat," said the Great Detective, "and let me know, in your own words, while omitting no detail, however slight, what has fetched you from the city of Washington in the District of Columbia to Baker Street in the city of London."

The President gave a violent start. "How do you know I'm from Wash—?" he began, when he was cut short impatiently by the Great Man:

"Tut, man, your boarding pass is sticking out of your pocket, apart from which those ears, made familiar to the point of despair by photographs in the daily newspapers, are too prominent to mistake. The case now, if you will."

"I have not the time to tarry," said the President, "busy as I am, conducting drone attacks on the civilian population with very occasional collateral damage to the real targets. Suffice to say that a neo-Keynesian who has been strenuously recommending a stimulus package for the economy has been found strenuously murdered in his study."

"Are the police," asked the Great Detective, "and the CIA and the FBI baffled beyond endurance? Does the case have international ramifications beyond imagination? If unsolved, will the case trigger World War III in the next 19-and-a-half hours? Does it involve some of the most distinguished names in America, Europe, and the rest of the world, or at least some of the less distinguished names? Do you have anything to add?"

"In response to your first four queries," replied the President, "Yes, yes, yes, and yes. In response to your fifth query, my intelligence sources advise me that the list of suspects has been narrowed down, for reasons we need not get into now, to three persons: a Syrian terrorist, the former President of the U.S., and a Professor of Economics at Chicago University. Your travel has been arranged, and I will be personally indebted to you if you should take the next flight to D.C. and investigate the case."

"Very well," said the Great Detective, adding, as he turned to me, "Pray pack a valise containing a few false beards, three pairs of goggles, twenty-three dressing gowns, my magnifying glass, the chemistry kit, a knife to skewer my correspondence with, a gasogene, a decanter, an Inverness cape, a deer-stalker, and some dog-biscuits for yourself."

In some hours, the Great Detective and I were in Washington, D.C. Upon his asking, the Great Detective was led to the murder victim's body in the mortuary. The Great Detective put on his deer-stalker, he affixed a green moustache to his upper-lip, and with the additional disguise of a red clown's nose, he threw himself upon the ground, sniffed the air, and crawled, on all fours, to the body, which he submitted to minute examination through the wrong end of his microscope. "Ha!" he said, his eyebrows waggling, his nose quivering, and his voice quavering, "Ha! Ho! Hum! Ha-ha!"

Suddenly, he flung himself up and unwinding his long, thin frame while simultaneously helping himself to a maroon moustache and a pair of pink glasses, he said: "That was a pretty three-pipe problem which I have succeeded in addressing with a single Meerschaum. The case is solved."

"My dear fellow! Who did it?"

"Obviously not the Syrian terrorist, since he has a perfect alibi by virtue of having been in Syria at the time of the murder. Observe the marks on the body, which clearly indicate that the victim has been murdered by first differentiating and equating to zero, and then differentiating again and confirming negativity.

The murder, obviously, has been perpetrated by a utility-maximizer, punctilious in the employment of both first- and second-order conditions for an extremum. We can immediately rule out the former President as a potential suspect: he can hardly be credited with engaging in the differential calculus when he has difficulty adding and spelling. Who, then, given to fanatical utility-maximization, might be expected to do violence to a neo-Keynesian economist, if not a Professor of Economics from Chicago? Hold him, before he escapes—!"

Unnoticed, the Chicago Economics Professor had followed us into the mortuary, but Inspector Lestrade (who had accompanied us from London) was too quick for him. "Would you?" he snarled, attaching himself to the sullen Professor's collar, as the latter tried to sneak away quietly.

Back in the White House, the Great Detective had the Presidential Medal pinned to his breast. He was also quickly conferred Membership of the American Academy of Arts and Sciences, and granted both the Oscar and Emmy Awards. "Is there," enquired the President, "anything further we can do to honour you? A special edition of *American Idol*, perhaps? A Hollywood extravaganza, maybe?"

"Tut, man," said the Great Detective carelessly. "The work is its own reward," and, turning to me, "If I may trouble you now for the syringe bearing a bolus of the good old seven per cent solution, followed by the papers of the Fotherington-Cholomondoley Succession Case and then the Featherstonehaugh-Beauchamp Forgery Case—? Ah, thank you."

The Conjurer's revenge

The audience had assembled to witness the Great Poverty Escape Act, conceived, sponsored, funded, and executed by the Global Magical Moneylenders' Guild of Reconstruction and Dissimulation under the inspiring leadership of the Great Conjurer, whose official designation was that of Head of the Research Committee of the Department of Mysteries in the Ministry of Magic (with registered country offices in the world-wide branches of the Hogwarts School of Witchcraft and Wizardry), aided by the services of the International Stooges' Federation of Hand-Waving Economeretricians.[1]

"Now, ladies and gentlemen," said the Great Conjurer, "I shall produce very little out of a great deal—902 million poor people in 2012 out of 1959 million poor people in 1980. We are ahead of schedule in meeting Millennium Development Goal 1. Presto!"

People everywhere in the audience were saying, "Oh, how marvelous! How did he do it?"

But the Quick Man on the front seat flung himself on his favourite idea and whispered madly in all directions: "He – had – a – particularly – low – poverty – line – up – his – sleeve."

A Leacockian view of economics today 51

And the people in the audience nodded sagely and sent the whisper flying to every corner of the hall: "He – had – an – extra-small – poverty – line – up – his – sleeve."

"My next trick," said the Great Conjurer, "is the famous Hindostanee Vanishing Numbers Trick. I shall now cut the Indian poverty headcount ratio by a further 20 per cent. *Choo mantar!* Also Presto!"

The audience reacted dazedly to this bold decapitation, until the Quick Man whispered: "He – had – a – sub-Tendulkar-Committee – Poverty – Line – up – his – sleeve." And everybody agreed and whispered: "Yes – he – had – a – sub-Tendulkar-Committee – Poverty – Line – up – his – sleeve."

The Great Conjurer's Olympian brow developed a furrow or two or three, as he continued: "I shall now amuse and entertain and gratify you with the Modified Hindostanee Vanishing Numbers Trick whereby I shall cut the Indian headcount ratio by an even more daring 10 per cent. Will one of the obliging Econometricians kindly lend me his wand? Ah—thank you—Presto!"

He cut the headcount ratio by a further 10 per cent, one per cent at a time, and for thirty-five seconds the audience was spell-bound, until the Quick Man whispered: "He – had – a – Modified – Mixed – Recall – Period – up – his – sleeve," and all the people in the audience passed it on: "He – had – a – Modified – Mixed – Recall – Period – up – his – sleeve."

The headcount trick was ruined.

Through the show, it went on like that. It transpired from the whispers of the Quick Man that the Great Conjurer must have had hidden up his sleeve, apart from a minuscule global poverty line, a sub-Tendulkar-Committee Poverty Line and a Modified Mixed Recall Period, also stacks and stacks of bogus Purchasing Power Parity equivalences, an entire Calorie Drift, several scores of country-specific Poverty Thresholds of which only the lowest 15 were used, a live (or at least only semi-moribund) poverty expert, an inventory of spurious regressions, hundreds of consumer price indices that failed to measure inflation, a Mainframe Super Computer capable of delivering a thousand doctored aggregate headcounts per second-squared, a full band for musical side-effects, a troop of cheerleaders, a copy of Harry Frankfurt's *On Bullshit*, and a crammer's guide to *Advanced Economicstricks*.

The Great Conjurer's and the Federation's reputations were in tatters. At the end of the show, the Great Conjurer made a final effort to salvage what he could of the evening.

"Ladies and gentlemen," he said, "I will now conclude the evening's entertainment with the celebrated Icelandic trick invented long ago by India's *tantric* votaries of *kundalini*, whereby," turning to the Quick Man with a smile of chillingly suave savagery, "I shall now, with this gentleman's permission, do indescribable things to his collar, his hat, his watch, and his coat. If I may, sir?"

"Of course you may," said the Quick Man with an affable smile, "but I can save everybody a lot of time and bother by confidently asserting that you will have done those indescribable things with the help of a cigarette lighter, a pair of gardening shears, a pair of dancing shoes, and a pot of green paint hidden – up – your – sleeve."

And once more the whisper went round the hall: "He – has – all – those – things – up – his – sleeve."

Amid a burst of dispirited music from the orchestra, the curtain descended upon the evening's edification, and the audience dispersed, convinced that there is not a trick in the book, especially when it comes to performing a Houdini Act on Global Poverty, which is not done up the Great Conjurer's sleeve.

"Q." A Psychic Pstory of the Psupernatural

What I am about to relate is the true but incredulous, by which I mean incredible, experience I had of phantasmal phinancial phlows in the ghastly gothic globalized world of ghostly go-betweens operating from beyond the grave. (These are examples of alluring alliterations, but that is another matter, whereas we are here concerned with the immaterial or spirit world, also known as the non-corporeal realm of miasmic manifestations, or perhaps something else.) Let me begin at the beginning, passing up the temptation of starting earlier. It began with my meeting A, on his invitation, in his chambers, at 4:52 P.M. precisely, on December the 23rd, a date and time which are graven in my memory if for no other reason than that I am not forgetful, either by nature or by design, assuming that means anything. A was a precise, unemotional, dry-voiced, dry-faced, drip-dried individual who worked in some mysterious import-export business that dealt, as far as one could tell, with things that were Free on Board or involved Cost, Insurance and Freight, Bills of Lading, and Letters of Credit. One would have scarcely associated this seemingly unimaginative and unsentimental man with astral phenomena or preternaturally paranormal events—with, in a word—ghosts, but then there we are.

In a quiet and even voice, A told me that his old, late friend (or late, old friend) Q, who had passed on (by which I mean expired) some years ago, seemed to be making an effort to get in touch with him, A, from the spirit world. "Addicted as Q had been to the world of shady transactions and tax havens all his adult corporeal life," A opined, "his premature death left in its wake a restless unsatiated spirit that would not rest quiescent in the knowledge of its unrealized potentialities for advancing the cause of illicit financial flows. I have been given an imitation, or intimation, of A's desire to get in touch with me. My attention was drawn from the reverie on illegal discounted cash flows into which I had fallen while sitting at my desk the other evening, by the sound of three sharp raps, as upon the table. Like this," added A, rapping the wooden desk sharply and causing me to bite my tongue and jump out of my skin. Re-entering my skin, I heard A relate the following singular tale:

"By projecting himself through the Ouija board of a psychic medium, Q was able to communicate with me. I could hear him tell me distinctly enough, through the crackling static of the nether world, the following: 'If you will arrange for my friend X to receive a million units of local currency, I will arrange, through the good offices of Z, to have the equivalent foreign exchange (at a premium, of course) in dollars transferred to a numbered account in Delaware, from where it will be distributed amongst several other numbered accounts, opened in the names of shell companies, in various banks in the Cayman Islands, the Channel Islands, the Isle of Man, Mauritius, the Guernsey and the Channel Islands, and Switzerland, all proxying for you, of course, my dear fellow. The funds can be repatriated, in a round-tripping arrangement, by way of bogus foreign investment. Just find those million units of local currency, and you will be in business.' The problem, of course, is that I am not a millionaire, whereas you are. How about it? Will you invest a million local currency units, at no risk to yourself and with the prospect of a premium-bearing foreign exchange return in the bargain, in the cause of advancing the frontiers of knowledge and experience beyond this constraining world of mere material possessions to the world of the spirit and the Great Beyond?"

For a moment I was spell-bound; for another moment, dumb-struck; and for a third moment, tongue-tied. Taking just one more moment off for speechlessness, I recovered my wits and my voice. "Why, of course I will," I replied. "It would be a pleasure to participate in this great scientific experiment!"

"Well then, meet me again with a million smackers tomorrow, same place, same time. Only, the transaction must be conducted entirely in cash." A lowered his voice as he said in a tone of affectionate recollection: "Q always dealt only in cash, and we don't want his sensitive spirit to be offended by negotiations through cheques, do we?"

"No, of course not," I said, in sympathetic identification.

Next day, I passed on a million notes in cash to A. I did not, of course, understand a word of what A said about Delaware and the Cayman Islands and numbered accounts and shell companies and round-tripping and foreign portfolio investment, but I gathered it was all in the cause of science and an alternative reality in the World Beyond. I was repeatedly struck by the strange and eerie significance of Q getting in touch with A to get in touch with me on the third day of every month of the subsequent six months, with the request, on each occasion, to come prepared to part with a million notes in cash, now for under-invoicing exports, now for over-invoicing imports, now for a spot of transfer-pricing, now for a dash of what A in a sepulchral voice said was financing trade in narcotics, and now again for a round of investment in human trafficking. As I have said, I had no notion of what all these financial transactions meant, except that they were part of this awesome experiment in establishing an ethereal reality, an experiment of which I was proud to be a part.

The culminating mystery occurred at the end of the sixth month. A vanished, as it were, into thin air, leaving no trace of his whereabouts (or of course of my millions). I was convinced that he had been sucked up in an osmotic force and into the void of the great spirit world, to be united once more and forever with his great friend Q. I was correct in my speculation. A few days hence I received a confirmatory telephone call. I heard A's voice, as if emanating from the pits of the alien world, assuring me that he was now with Q in another country of the spirit. He counseled me not to mourn my lost millions, for it had all been in a great and wonderful cause. I was then, and continue to remain, convinced that A was a martyr to the experiment he had conducted with such courage and steadfastness, and that my experience was but a testament to his commitment to the truth.

After all, and as he assured me, my millions were but a paltry fraction of the twenty-five trillion dollars that had escaped the developing world in illicit financial flows.

A hero in homespun: or, the life struggle of Hezekiah Hayloft

The Chairman of the Department also occupied the Chair of Advanced Mathematical Economics and Economic Theory. It was on this Chair that he was sitting when a fresh-faced lad entered his study. It was Hezekiah Hayloft. Hezekiah was entirely in homespun. Hezekiah also carried a carpet-bag in each hand, and the notion in his head that it was a good idea to come to New York in search of an education that would make him an economist capable of understanding and solving the problems of poverty and inequality and unemployment and inflation. He asked the Chairman if he might register for a Ph.D. under him. The Chairman found something engaging in the lad's wistful expression. It might almost be said that he saw his own younger self of long ago in the person standing before him. He threw an ink-pot at him, and him out of the study.

Wandering down the corridor, Hezekiah encountered the college Chaplain and enquired if he, the Chaplain, would pray for him, Hezekiah, to find a berth in the Department to do research on social security for the poor. The Chaplain, in a voice inarticulate with rage, said something about how the wretched lad would be better off studying the properties of unstable equilibria in epsilon environments, but seeing that he was incapable, the Chaplain said that what was indicated was not so much prayer as a good hiding and, suiting the action to the word, he set violently upon Hezekiah and beat the stuffing out of him.

The Chaplain, in his old age, was less thorough than he had been in his youth. He hated to leave a job half done. He entrusted the completion of the commission to the janitor. The janitor was happy to suck Hezekiah up in his vacuum cleaner and then spit him out.

Dejected but not defeated, Hezekiah wandered further down the corridor and buttonholed one of the three Nobel laureates the Department boasted. Expressing a desire to study the importance of the minimum wage for worker welfare, he was confronted by the query, addressed in a voice of thunder by the laureate, whether Hezekiah could handle Haufsdorff dimensions and Banach spaces in the cause of demonstrating the uniqueness of stable steady states in the core of a competitive economy yielded by the non-degenerate intersection of n-manifolds. Hezekiah answered truthfully: "I can often add with varying success, occasionally subtract, and more rarely do a sum in long division. But I am prepared to work hard and learn." The laureate, thereupon, chewed off his ear, kicked him several times in the hind-quarters, and sent him on his way—but not before he had arranged for Hezekiah to run the gauntlet of the Department's twenty-one graduate students, of whom three were female all-in wrestlers specializing in subgame perfect coalition proof Nash equilibria.

Gradually, with the passage of time and repeated exposure to insults, kicks, bites, dusters, and ink-pots, a change came over the lad: he became embittered and hardened. Thrusting his substantial jaw out, he muttered to himself: "I will succeed yet, by foul means if not fair; yes I will—by Jupiter, by Friedman, by Barro, by Muth!" So saying, he systematically broke into the rooms of the senior faculty and stole all the results of their work in progress.

Before he knew it, Hezekiah was in possession of 132 lemmata and 193 theorems on the super-neutrality of money, the inefficacy of fiscal stimulus, the efficacy of macroeconomic stabilization and structural adjustment, the necessity of debt-recovery by force and violence, the hyper-optimality of unfair trade practices, the multidimensional nature of lies about global poverty, and the incentive-compatible uniqueness of growth equilibria without foreign aid. What is more, he boldly published his stolen results in the most prestigious journals of the day. He was hired by several supra-national institutions such as the Global Bank, the International Trade Organization, and the World Monetary Fund to destroy several developing economies, which he did. His success knew no bounds. His reputation grew and grew. It was only a matter of time before he was offered permanent tenure in the departments of several Ivy League colleges, which vied desperately with each other to hire him, and bid his remuneration up in the bargain. The very men who had sneered at him now grovelled at his feet. It was Hezekiah who now brandished the ink-pots.

To keep his reputation going, Hezekiah had to hire several research assistants and graduate students, from all of whom he stole his ideas and his scientific papers. When one of the students delayed the proof of a lemma, Hezekiah shot him through the waistcoat. He came to stand his trial in court. The prosecuting attorney, the witnesses, the judge, the jury, and the press were all very sympathetic to Hezekiah. The court found in his favour and awarded him damages. However, the verdict was challenged in the Supreme Court on a writ of *mandamus*, followed by a writ of *certiori*. There the case now stands, at the end of twenty-three years and 1,912 adjournments.

Meanwhile, Hezekiah was appointed President of Halfward University, whose funds he speculated with for his private gain and which he sensibly invested in the cause of his election to the State Senate.

Hezekiah Hayloft's life struggle will soon culminate with his election as President of the country.

THE END

Note

1 Martin Gardner is rumoured to have been present at the Federation's naming ceremony.

//
Part III
On institutions, culture, and society

8 Learning economics and the law anew

Notes for the reader

It would appear that the present values informing economics are actually values of great vintage that trace their way back to our ancient texts and treatises. Likewise, the law, apparently, is a thicket of incomprehensible language, access to which is confined only to the learned, and kept securely away from the polluting grasp of the unwashed and the illiterate, even as knowledge in our days of old was the exclusive preserve of the wise and the pure. These themes are explored in what follows.

Vedanomics

There has, in the recent past, been a spate of invidious and seriously misguided commentaries on the allegedly anachronistic and unscientific allusions made by politicians of a certain persuasion to bodies of knowledge in Vedic antiquity that anticipated several 'modern' scientific theories in medicine and physics, among other disciplines.

A common and deplorable feature informing these 'critiques' has been a combination of motivated prejudice, uncouth satire, pseudo-secular arrogance, cultural deracination, woefully inadequate scholarship, and anti-national sentiment.

This is reflected, for instance, in crude jokes and treasonable attacks that have been made upon the historical origins of such subjects as plastic surgery, general relativity, the aero-dynamics of flight, and genetic engineering. In the rough-and-tumble of politics, speakers addressing lay (or specialist) audiences can scarcely be expected to find the time for scholarly annotations of their statements, with detailed references to chapter, verse, and original text.

This wholly excusable omission in the cause of informal discourse and dialogue with subjects who are regarded with friendly sympathy by the speaker as idiots has regrettably been seized upon by critics to pour scorn and doubt upon the justifiably claimed pre-eminence of Vedic thought in the realm of science. This is a scandal, and the record cries out to be set right.

Indeed, it is not just the natural and life sciences which can trace their provenance back to Vedic times and texts, but also disciplines in the social and behavioural sciences, such as economics, politics, and psychology. This very brief contribution is aimed at affirming this truth and negating some of the orchestrated efforts that have been made to tarnish it.

What follows is a short and select bibliography of relevant Vedic sources for certain modern themes in the social and behavioural sciences.

One is able, at best, to provide only rough dates for these sources: among other things, these texts and treatises are frequently the work, performed over time, of several hands, and it is never a simple matter to trace authorship back to some single identifiable person. The reader is invited to contrast this with the approved practice of uniquely attributing, say, the differential calculus to Isaac Newton, who actually stole it, via Gottfried Leibnitz, from the Kerala Mathematical School (c. 1300–1500 C.E.).

In economics, both demonetisation and goods-and-services-taxation were systematically anticipated in the thesis (c. 1000–900 B.C.E.) titled *Praja Sampoorna-nāśa Prakarana* (*Treatise on the Comprehensive Destruction of a Country's Subjects*, trans. von Böhtlingk: Dordrecht, 1889), and commonly attributed to the worldly philosopher Narendra Bhattathiri.

The economics of land-acquisition is dealt with in *Daridrabhūmicauryavr̥ttiśāstra* (1800 B.C.E.; trans. Max Mueller: 'The Science of Stealing Land from the Poor,' *Zeitschrift für Sanskrit*, 1872).

The economics of child-work is well covered in the 600 B.C.E. tract *Bālakarmanvidohakalā* (*The Art of Exploiting a Child's Labour*, trans. Pandit Brijbhushan Girdharilal Tripathi: Premier Lotus Heritage Books, Gorakhpur, 1937, further edited, and with annotations, by Pa Su Mahadeva Dikshitar, Thirumangalakudi Vedapatasala, 1939).

The ancient (and anonymous) text (c. 2300 B.C.E.) titled *āhūtaprapalāyinvijñāna* is the locus classicus on 'Techniques of Absconding.'

The *Lokatantravipralambhana*, which Ernst Heinrich Meier translated as *The Frauds of Democracy*, can be more loosely (and usefully) rendered as *Disqualifying Legislators*; and the anonymous 800 B.C.E. treatise *Vitathavādin* (literally, 'Lying') was plagiarised and published in 1923 as *Propaganda* by Joseph Goebbels.

It would call for some generosity of spirit—or, less demandingly, an ordinary deference to facts—to acknowledge that several aspects of government policy, legislation, and practice in the present dispensation have reflected an inspiriting loyalty to the credo of our Vedic texts, which it is a simple matter to invent where they do not exist.

Above all, it should be an event of pride for all Indians that Keynes himself once acknowledged the debt owed by his *General Theory of Employment, Interest and Money* to Vedic Economics. This is a true statement, even if subsequent verification with the Estate of John Maynard Keynes should elicit a denial.

Justice for all, comprehension for none

No one should be seriously surprised if, in the not-too-distant future, an event should occur and some such report on it as the following one were to make its appearance in the print media:

'A group calling themselves Citizens of India recently filed a case in the Supreme Court against the justices of the Court. The petition accused some of the judges of violating the principle of "Justice for All" by writing judgements which could not be understood by anybody, including in particular the authors of the verdicts. This suit was filed in the aftermath of an important judgement delivered in a case of great constitutional significance which ran to more than 500 pages and whose opening sentence alone took up 119 words.

'Petitioner's claim was that of the 29,032 members of the group called Citizens of India who attempted to read the judgement, 89.02% could not proceed beyond the Prologue for reasons of extreme mental exhaustion, 7.69% lapsed into a coma from near-terminal neural drainage, and 3.29% expired from instantaneous paralytic incomprehension.

'It is learnt informally that the justices who presided over the case are furious over the fact that the Citizens of India are still at large though they were sentenced (in the cause of the country's collective conscience) to death by hanging for displaying disrespect to the judges and contempt for the court.

'The sentence, it is understood, has not been carried out because nobody could comprehend the operational part of the judgement (nor indeed any other part of it).

'Reproduced below is a minuscule fraction of the 783-page judgement written by the Chief Justice on behalf of himself and his four colleagues constituting the 5-judge bench that heard the case. (By way of a word of caution, the excerpt below could have severe—including fatal—side effects on senior citizens who think they know English, patients with a history of heart disease, excitable individuals, and people of every other demographic description.)

> In the Supreme Court of India
> Civil Appellate Jurisdiction
> Citizens of India . . . Appellant
> Versus
> Hon. Judges of Supreme Court . . . Respondents

Prologue

1   This vexed and vexatious question, a query informed by the interrogative faculty of *homo sapiens*, is sought to be aired in the forum of public interest, designed for and designated by the class of claims known as human rights, in what is purported to be a bold and unpusillanimous blow for the expressive freedom of expression at the dispensing end

of *verbis legal* to be expressly matched by the impressive freedom of interpretative and instructional internalisation at the receiving end of *communi sermone*, in order that an exciting and excruciating balance might be struck between the demands and tensions and perceivedly oppositional forces of the Language of the Law and the Language of the Common Man (whose wife, sister, and mother, may it be said in deference to the superior exaltation of the female of the species, are examples of the Uncommon Woman).

2   Couched thus in the democratic ambience of reasoned and reasonable demand, this interrogative interrogation questions the propriety and meaning, not to say the hermeneutic interpretability and effect potentiality, of the prose in which is fashioned, by my learned colleagues—each one a master and a magister of the word whether it be articulated in the divine gift of speech or the sacred form of holy writ—those precious gems, those Tanzanites and Grandidierites and Jadeites, of jurisprudential wisdom distilled as it is in the essence of legal acumen, crystallised as it in the liquid clarity of experiential justice, and sanctified, not to say sacralised, as it is by the purity of Constitutional and, indeed, constitutive knowledge, a knowledge that transcends the understanding of the *hoi polloi*, even as it vaults over the high bar of such learned construal as can be achieved even by the highest authorities of discourse-mediated verbalisation.

3   To thus convey opprobrium of the penmanship involved in the ostentatiously ornate organisation of the juridical oeuvre and opus of an adjudicatory authority and interpretatory intercessor is an act that may convey a false and fallacious sense of democratic deliberation premised on the extenuatingly exquisite grounds of equal or at least not unequal equality before the law, but stands exposed, laid bare, revealed, and denounced as an act that is as apparently appropriate as it is really reprobate, as seemingly seemly as it is indubitably insolent, and as phenomenally pious as it is noumenally nefarious, for such opprobrium is craftily concealed in the beguiling beatitude of pious parity and counter-balanced commensurateness which constitute the misconceivedly mendacious ethic of the equality of unequals and serve directly to initiate a process of litigation that deserves the severest condemnation as nugatory, frivolous, and ultimately contumacious, arising from which it would be prudent for petitioner to herewith and forthwith absquatulate—

'This reporter is afraid he is unable to proceed further: the machine on which he has been working has just flashed a warning on the monitor, which reads: "There will be an explosion if the content management system is expected to process any more of this ****." This reporter has had to resort to "****" because even his restricted knowledge of the law suggests it is very likely that the word is ultimately contumacious.'

9 The adventures of 'Chalak' Om, as chronicled by Dr Vatsan

Athur Kannan Thayyil

Notes for the reader

These are records of some of the cases handled by Dr Vatsan's illustrious friend and colleague, the consulting detective Om Prakash, known to an admiring public as 'Chalak' Om on account of his astuteness and acumen in uncovering mysteries. Since he specialised in cases relating to fraud, bribery, corruption, chicanery and all manner of sharp practice, ministers and bureaucrats and the police were not always his best friends, though it is amazing how often they consulted him. This they did whenever they thought he might be of help in uncovering evidence that could fix their political or professional rivals. The stories, it is hoped, will have some instructive value regarding our society's present values.

The case of the missing aircraft

My notes indicate that it was on a certain wintry December afternoon of the year '18 that I found myself once more in front of our old *barsati* at b122 Bekar Street, the starting point of so many remarkable adventures I have had in the company of my friend Mr 'Chalak' Om. I find it recorded in my scribbled memo that I was having difficulty breathing that day on account of Delhi's polluted air. (I find the same thing recorded also for every other day of the year. In a year or two after that, we learnt to stop breathing in order to cope with the situation.)

As I let myself into Om's (and my former) apartment with a spare key, another individual emerged from within. Despite the fact that he had on a pair of dark glasses which covered his eyes, I could tell—so shifty-eyed was he—that the man was seriously shifty-eyed. We passed each other, he on his way out and I on my way in.

I found my friend stretched out on his sofa, his head in a swirl of smoke from the countless *bidis* he had smoked during the day. The pollution of the air outside the two-room *barsati* was precisely balanced by the pollution

64 On institutions, culture, and society

of the air inside. Even as I entered, Om reached for another of the noxious Langar Chhap Bidis which he kept in a Jodhpur slipper, and which he helped himself to from time to time.

"I know you don't approve, my dear fellow," he observed sardonically. "But one day you will thank me for adapting you to a life without oxygen. Be that as it may," he said, eyeing me keenly, "I see that you have been reading the political headlines of the day."

"How on earth did you guess, Om—?" said I in amazement.

"Tut, man, it is simplicity itself. The look of utter disgust on your face gives away the activity you have been recently engaged in. Nothing can produce quite that look of repugnance and loathing on a man's face as the political news of the day which our country has to offer. And by the way, I never guess: it is a shocking habit. Setting that aside, what did you make of the fellow who just passed you at the doorway?"

"A client, no doubt?"

"No doubt. And a client from where, would you say? You know my methods, Vatsan: apply them!"

"I would hazard the surmise that he was a Central Bureau of Intelligence official."

"Capital, Vatsan! And how did you deduce that?"

"Well, anybody as shifty-eyed as that, despite the protective camouflage of heavily tinted glasses, must belong to an Intelligence agency!"

"Bravo! I see that your years with me have not been wasted!"
"But which CBI is he from—CBI-1 or CBI-2?"
"You are behind the times, Vatsan. The CBI has now splintered into 32 factions, and my recent client belongs to the group that calls itself CBI-21. He is interested in fixing a hated rival in CBI-7 on allegations of sabotaging the investigation into the Rifle Aircraft deal. The deal, you will recall, was initially for 126 aircraft, but that has now been whittled down to just 36 aircraft. CBI-21 is interested in knowing how 90 of the aircraft disappeared into thin air, as it were."
"And how indeed did they disappear?"
"Through long division, my dear fellow. 126 divided by 36 is 3.5. If the price of each aircraft is increased by three-and-a-half times, the number of aircraft will dwindle from 126 to 36."
"But why was the price raised?"
"To accommodate India-specific enhancements, according to CBI-7. To finance the investment of the dud Indian off-set partner and so save him from bankruptcy, according to CBI-21."
"And which one is right?"
"Our voters will decide that at the General Elections. Meanwhile, there is the bell, heralding a new client. When you open the door to let him in, Vatsan, you will encounter a fellow in dark glasses identical to the chap you let out some minutes ago. This fellow, as we will discover, is the Chief of CBI-7, who will consult me on how he can fix the Chief of CBI-21 for interfering in his investigation."
"What will you do, Om?"
"Why, I'll take on both their cases and pocket both their fees and let them slug each other to a standstill. If you will wait for a half-hour to see CBI-7 out, then we can do something purposive with the evening. Ustad Amjad Ali Khan is performing tonight, and we can follow that up with a spot of dinner at Moti Mahal. What say you, Vatsan?"
"Need you ask, Om? Anywhere and anytime, my dear fellow!"

The adventure of the vanished governor

Readers will recall the mysterious circumstances under which the head of one of the country's most important institutions suddenly disappeared in the early winter of the year '19. Few, if any of them, are aware of the role played by my distinguished friend Mr 'Chalak' Om in the mystery. With the passage of time, the details of that singular episode can now at last be revealed to an eager and expectant public.

The first intimation of the case I had was when I returned home one late winter's evening from my rounds, to the *barsati* I had resumed sharing with my friend at b122 Bekar Street. On letting myself in through the front door, I was surprised to discover a familiar-looking stranger in consultation with 'Chalak' Om. Muttering a hasty apology, I made to move toward my bedroom when Om stopped me with these words: "Pray join us, if that is convenient, Vatsan. My client was just about to present his case when you entered. You will have no difficulty in recognising our illustrious client. This, sir, is Dr Vatsan, before whom you may be as candid as you would be with me: I expect that his assistance will be invaluable."

Our client was indeed an illustrious personage. I had no difficulty in recognising him from the satisfied smile he wore on his face, and which I had witnessed so often on television at the presentation of every Annual Budget over the last few years. It was the Economics Minister himself.

"You must know, Mr Om," began the Minister, "that the decision on demonetisation was not taken in a hurry. It was intended to mop up the black money in the system, or at least to formalise the informal economy, or at least to hasten the transition to digitisation, or at least none of the above, in which—you will concede—we have succeeded most admirably. To suggest anything else is a canard beyond description, and is the handiwork of an opposition that supports urban naxals and cannot trace its *gotra*. I would be inclined to say the same thing about the Goods and Services Tax, and Smart Cities and the Bullet Train—"

Om, who had been leaning back in his armchair with his eyes closed and his fingers steepled, suddenly opened his eyes. Sometimes he could be very austere and forbidding, as he was now. Fixing his client with a penetrating stare, he said: "You strangely forget your audience, Economics Minister. You are not addressing a political rally. Rather, you are speaking to a consulting detective and his side-kick on a matter which you suggested was a matter of urgent national importance. Pray come to the point. I fear that with elections around the corner, you are overwrought. You need something to steady your nerves. Perhaps you would like to try one of my *bidis*? Langar Chhap that side, Ganesh Bidis this."

The Economics Minister declined the offer with a shudder that shook his body from stem to stern. "My apologies for not coming straightaway to the point, Mr Om. We at the Ministry need your services in locating the Governor of the Reverse Bank of India. He vanished without a trace last evening. The Reverse Bank is now rudderless."

"That, I would have imagined," murmured Om, "is surely in the interests of the banking system."

"Ha, ha, Mr Om," tittered the Minister politely. "On the other hand, there are matters of the most vital necessity and immediate urgency on which the

The adventures of 'Chalak' Om 67

Ministry needs to consult him, and it is severely discommoding to us that the Governor is nowhere to be found."

"Rest assured, Economics Minister," said Om soothingly, "I am seized of the gravity of the situation. I have one or two thoughts on where the Governor of the Reverse Bank may be found. Let me explore these leads. I shall get back to you on the subject just as soon as I am in a position to report some encouraging news to you. Meanwhile, Vatsan here will see you through to the front door."

I returned to the armchair after seeing the Minister out. "Well, Om, what do you make of it?" I asked my friend. By way of response, he rapped the side of the armchair, and said in a high-pitched voice: "It is safe to emerge now." I was amazed to see a human form crawl out from under Om's armchair. It was the Governor of the Reverse Bank of India!

"Surely you are abetting a felony, Om!" I cried.

"It is no felony to allow a man to crawl under one's armchair, Vatsan. The Governor justifiably wishes to avoid having pressure exerted on him by the Minister to transfer his Bank's accumulated reserves to the Ministry. So I have advised him to lie low for a few days, which he has chosen to interpret in a somewhat literal-minded way by crawling under my armchair. A few days of absence is a scandal which should jolt the Ministry; and when he makes a reappearance, I doubt the Governor will be subjected to any further harassment to part with the Bank's reserves. Over the next three days, the Governor will share your bedroom with you."

Alas! The best-laid plans of mice and men. . . . The Governor managed to give us the slip on his second day of refuge. Feeling in urgent need of a savoury snack, he slipped out of b221, only to be spotted, nabbed, and whisked away by the authorities from the *bhel puri* shop on the intersection of Bekar Street and Parthaman Square. His nerves thoroughly shattered by now, he submitted his resignation immediately, much to the relief of the Economics Minister.

Om blamed me bitterly for taking my eye off the Governor, which I thought was very unfair. Nevertheless, to make light of the issue, it occurred to me to make a bit of a joke of the matter, which I am afraid did not go very well with Om.

"I wish, Om," said I, "that you would have taken the precaution to 'URGE IT' upon him to refrain from sneaking out of the *barsati*. Did you get it?—I mean the pun on the words 'URGE IT'—"

"I can occasionally brook your pawky wit, Vatsan, but I find your sense of humour has lately been descending to execrably infantile depths," said Om coldly. "And now, if you will be so good as to hand over the papers of the Niksi-Chorav Embezzlement Papers to me—"

The adventure of the absconding defaulters

As I dragged myself sleepily one morning into the drawing room of our *barsati* in b122 Bekar Street, I found that my friend 'Chalak' Om was already up and about. Indeed, it turned out that he had not slept all night. Our landlady's *aloo-paratha* breakfast lay untouched upon the table, while the floor by the room-heater was littered with a mounting pile of Langar Chhap *bidis*. Om himself was sitting cross-legged and motionless upon his armchair, his eyes closed in deep contemplation.

"A case, my dear fellow?" I ventured to ask.

Om opened his eyes and regarded me without favour. "Yes, a case, Vatsan. A side-kick should be of some assistance—by serving as a sounding-board, if nothing else. Can you at least offer me your undivided attention, without the distraction of an interminable breakfast?"

"Very well, Om," I said, a trifle nettled by his tone. "I was only into my sixth cup of coffee and my eighth *aloo-paratha*—but I'm prepared to accept a certain order of starvation if it will help you with your case."

"As you are aware, the Central Bureau of Intelligence has now splintered into 32 factions. CBI-21 is one of the only two groups that are interested in (occasionally) fighting crime and solving cases that are referred to the Agency. Late last night, Inspector L—of CBI-21 was here—inspired as much by the ambition of upstaging his hated rival Inspector G—of CBI-7 as anything else—to seek my advice on tracking down three persons, former associates of the arch-criminals Niksi and Chorav, who had defaulted, to the tune of several thousand crores, on loans borrowed from the Bank of Allahabad. A CBI operative who was involved in the man-hunt has managed to track the absconders down to three cities in Uttar Pradesh. He sent an e-mail message to Inspector L—, which reads as follows: 'I know where the absconders are. They are in the cities of Gomukheshwar, Ramganga, and Antardesh.' Inspector L—immediately shot off a response: 'Can't find referenced cities on map. Kindly clarify.' Back came the reply from the field operative. 'Didn't want message to be intercepted by hackers, so employed code of Jellystone Park's bear.' Before further clarification could be sought, the field operative was found murdered in the most mysterious circumstances. The absconders' friends and promoters are suspected to be behind the killing. Inspector L— has left me with the task of deciphering his late operative's code."

"Was it really necessary to use a code?" I asked.

"What do you mean, was it really necessary," said my companion testily. "This is a 'Chalak' Om story, is it not? Are there any other ways in which you propose to make yourself useless?"

"Several," I retorted, finally stung by Om's rudeness. "Here, by way of example, is one such unhelpful question. Shouldn't the Bank of Allahabad

now be called the Bank of Prayag, after the recent re-naming by the Uttar Pradesh Chief Minister?"

For a moment, Om stared at me, before gripping my arm warmly. "I must congratulate you, my dear fellow," he cried. "You have solved the case, though—it goes without saying, of course—you have no notion of having done so!"

"Why, what do you mean, Om?" I stammered.

"Consider, Vatsan, who is the Bear of Jellystone Park?"

"It is that cartoon character Yogi Bear, is it not?"

"Superb! And who has recently been changing the names of cities in Uttar Pradesh?"

"The Yogi, surely!" I exclaimed.

"Precisely!" said Om. "In the Yogi's code, the cities of Gomukheshwar, Ramganga, and Antardesh would be the mythological equivalents of cities that were probably named under Mughal rule. All we need to do is to locate the equivalents. Quick, Vatsan, the Index! What have we here on cities with Islamic names? Fassbinder—Fatal—Fatehpur: now then, speculated to be the Antardesh of Vedic times! Gasogene—Ghalib—ah! Here we are: Ghaziabad, believed to be the Gomukheshwar of mythology! And Moplah—Morabba—Ho! Hum!—Good Old Index! Moradabad: built on the banks of the river Ramganga! That is where L—'s men should find the absconders: in Fatehpur, Ghaziabad, and Moradabad! I'll let L—know straightaway."

The following morning, Om tossed across a telegram to me. It was from Inspector L—of CBI-21. It read: "Absconders nabbed at Fatehpur, Ghaziabad, and Moradabad. Much obliged to you."

"To *you*, he should have said, my dear fellow," said Om generously. "I think we deserve to give ourselves a treat. Do you have any suggestions?"

"I believe I know the very place for it, Om: a *jalebi* enterprise located on Dariba Kalan ('The Incomparable Pearl') Road, if you are interested in a hot, dripping dessert."

"That sounds splendid, Vatsan. It is possible, though, that by the time we get there, your *jalebi-wala* will no longer be on Dariba Kalan Road, but on Apurva Gutika Road—or, who knows, on Apratimāna Mauktika Sarani— but come, let us be on our way: *jalebi* is *jalebi* whether the shop is on a road with a Persian name or a Sanskrit one!"

The return of the dancing men

On going through my notes for the twelve-month of the year March '18– March '19, I find instances of several cases of the greatest interest which challenged, and were eventually compelled to yield to, the formidable

The adventures of 'Chalak' Om   71

powers of reasoning and analytical acumen that were so signal a feature of the long and distinguished forensic career of my friend Mr 'Chalak' Om. Here I find a reference to the Case of the Defamed Tycoon, and there a reference to the Case of the Entrance Examination; here a mention of the Adventure of the Fugitive Jewellers, and there an allusion to the Affair of the Politician's Son; here an account of the Case of the Alert(ed) Absconders, and there a record of the Case of the Un-taxed Godman.

At a general level, all of these remarkable cases pointed to the abiding nutritional mystery of the expanding waistlines of a category of people who were rumoured neither to eat nor allow their friends to eat. It is not, however, of this set of cases that I now propose to write. Of an altogether different order of appeal from these enigmas of digestive anomaly was the bizarre and *outré* case of the Reappearance of the Dancing Men, which I trust will prove to be of some interest to the reading public.

Upon my return from my evening practice to our lodgings in b122 Bekar Street on a very cold January day of the year '19, I found that a client was engaged in deep and earnest conversation with 'Chalak' Om. On Om's insistence that I should join the consultation, it was revealed to me that our client was the Union Minister of Unlawful Activities, and that he had come to seek Om's advice on a sensitive case which was of concern to as many as ten agencies that operated under his Ministry—the Brainpower Department, the Dope Regulation Bureau, the Coercion Directorate, the Central Bureau of Forthright Taxes, the Inspectorate of Revenue Brainpower, the Central Bureau of Snooping, the National Snooping Agency, the Closet Secretariat, the Inspectorate of Signal Brainpower, and the Delhi Department of Police.

These agencies, it may be recalled by keen followers of certain aspects of the government's policy initiatives of the times, had been authorised to engage in activities relating to the interception, monitoring, and decryption of any information generated, transmitted, received, or stored in any computer resource under the Information Technology Act of 2000.

Om, who had been attending to the Minister's deposition with rapt attention, opened his eyes briefly to say: "The Government Order in question, which empowers you to snoop on your citizens with impunity, should be a source of the greatest pleasure to you. You appear despondent, when you ought to be rubbing your palms in anticipation of the joys of administering the third degree to hundreds upon thousands of anti-national citizens."

"Aye, Mr Om, there's the rub o' it," said the statesman. (Not that the Minister spoke like that, but we must preserve the atmosphere of a proper 'Chalak' Om story.) "We have reason to believe, you see, that one or more of the ten agencies I have mentioned has left behind footprints of an act of treason, which we wish you to investigate and identify."

"Footprints, Minister? A man's or a woman's?"

The Minister's voice sank to a hoarse, dramatic whisper, barely audible above the sound of the unseasonal winter rain falling with insistence upon the roof of the *barsati*: "They are the footprints, Mr Om, of a gigantic mole."

Om knit his brows in impatience. "Minister, you speak in metaphorical riddles. Pray be so good as to state the nature of the problem as clearly and straightforwardly as you can."

"Well, it is like this, Mr Om," explained the Minister. "We have drawn up plans for snoo—er—intercepting the email messages of (as you put it) hundreds of thousands of people whom our agencies have identified as Urban Naxals. We have every reason to believe that there is a mole in the apple who has leaked this information to our target suspects."

"And what evidence have you for this?"

"Mr Om, the only email or Facebook message that has been sent to their respective correspondents by our suspected Urban Naxals over the last twenty-four hours is this bizarre frieze of dancing men." At this point, the Minister fished out a computer printout from his pocket, which he handed over to Om, who shared it with me. Here is a reproduction of the singular set of hieroglyphs that Om held in his hand:

"This is obviously a sinister code intended to signal some dastardly message to the Enemy," said the Minister. "Can you decode it, Mr Om?"

"Well, well," said Om, his eyes glinting and his body racked with paroxysms of internal mirth. "There is no great mystery here, Minister. The Code of the Dancing Men was deciphered over a hundred years ago by my illustrious forbear Mr Sherlock Holmes of Baker Street. This should have been apparent to you and to the personnel of your ten agencies of Snooping and Brainpower if only any of you had been acquainted with the singular case of 'The Adventure of the Dancing Men,' as recorded by Dr Watson in *The Return of Sherlock Holmes*. Each of the dancing men, you would have realised, stands for a letter of the English alphabet.

"What you have in the cipher, then, are groups of letters making up words separated one from the other by a dancing man holding up a flag. In the message in front of you, you have two words: the first has four letters and the second three. It is only the last of the dancing men, drawn twice over, as you will see, that has not already been decoded by Mr Holmes.

"As for the remaining symbols, reading from right to left, they stand (as Mr Holmes' decryption should show) for the letters 'O,' 'S,' 'S,' 'I,' and 'P.' Your message, then, reads: PISS O_ _. I fancy we would be justified in assigning the letter 'F' to the last dancing man. Fully decoded, the message in front of you is the injunction to 'PISS OFF.'"

"What can it mean, Mr Om? To whom is it addressed?" asked the Minister.

"You supplied the answer yourself, Minister. The message is addressed to the Enemy—and surely you recognise yourself and your agencies in the Enemy? As for what it means, tell me, sir: what would you say to somebody who opened your mail, and read your private correspondence, and poked their noses into your personal affairs, and then used these as a basis for punishing you simply because you disagreed with them?"

"Why," said the Minister, "I suppose I should say something like 'Piss Off.' Or something even more rudimentary, but in similar vein."

"Ah," said Om, "having been tipped off by an Urban Naxal in one of your agencies, all the other targeted Urban Naxals have got together to let you and your Snooping Agencies know what they think of you—and is doing so, they have said precisely what you admit you yourself would have said if your respective positions had been reversed. Really, Minister, I should learn something from this if I were you. After all: *Vox Populi, Vox Dei*. Would you not agree?

"And now, I shall be happy to pocket that cheque for Rs. 50 lakh which you had promised for the unravelling of the code of the dancing men. I am a poor man, and it is shocking how much inflation your official price data conceal."

The adventure of the five amla seeds

From among the innumerable cases filed by his trusted Boswell in his archives, there are a few investigated by my friend 'Chalak' Om that had outcomes which he neither promoted nor prevented, but merely deciphered and foretold. A typical member of this category of cases is well represented by the singular event of the Five Amla Seeds which may now be disclosed with the passage of time and which will, I trust, enable readers to finally acquire an insight into the circumstances leading to the extraordinary governance of the county's major institutions in the months immediately preceding the General Elections of the year '19.

It was on an unseasonably cold morning of early March in the capital city that the case in question was first brought to our attention. Our landlady Mrs Hardhan was a kindly and gifted provider of nourishment whose efforts were often wasted on Om's spare and meagre appetite, for which deficiency I felt called upon to compensate: it was, accordingly, as I was putting away the last of twenty-two *idlis* at breakfast that morning that the first of what proved to be a regular retinue of distinguished clients, all of them heads of one or other of this country's major institutions, made their appearance at b122 Bekar Street.

Our first visitor was the Prime Justice of the Apex Court, who arrived in a state of considerable agitation. Om, in his customary soothing manner, had no sooner seated the Justice in the armchair by the room heater and lit a Langar Chhap *bidi*, and closed his eyes and steepled his fingers in anticipation of his client's deposition, than there was an interruption. Overriding Mrs Hardhan's futile efforts at restraining him, the door was flung open to admit a second seriously agitated visitor who proved to be the Governor of the Reverse Bank of India. In less than no time, he was followed, in that order, by a shaken Chairperson of the Media Trust, a stirred Chief of the Central Vigilante Commission, a quivering Chief of the Central Misinformation Commission, and a trembling Head of the Ballot Commission.

It did not take long, under Om's masterful handling of the situation, to gather that all of the dignitaries had come to consult him in connection with an identical occurrence that each of them had experienced that morning. The facts can be briefly related as follows. Each of our visitors had found upon his breakfast table an envelope addressed to him. The envelopes bore no postal marks, having evidently been delivered by hand. Each envelope

The adventures of 'Chalak' Om 75

contained a folded message enclosing five dried amla seeds. (For the benefit of 'Chalak' Om's overseas admirers, let me clarify that an amla is an Indian gooseberry.) The message, typed in bold letters, conveyed the following chilling intimation: 'THIS IS YOUR FIRST, LAST, AND FINAL WARNING.' Each message was signed off with a 'ψ.'

"An assignment executed by Maurya, R. T.'s organisation, if I am any judge of these matters," said Om. "The man's tentacles spread far and wide, and it would have been no difficulty for his agents to suborn some member of the domestic staff in each of you dignitaries' households and get him or her to deliver the note with its contents. Be that as it may, why have you come to me? Surely you should have consulted the police on this matter, or our premier National Snooping Agency?"

The dignitaries shuffled their feet and shifted their eyes. "Ah," said Om, "You do not trust our snoopers . . . nor each other, I should imagine. Nor do I wonder," he added in a marked manner, following a deliberate study of the delegates' countenances. "Well, well, not that it matters. I have been expecting him for some time now, and here, if I mistake not, is his step upon the stair—." Even as Om spoke, the door burst open once more, the Director of the Central Snooping Bureau staggered in, waved an envelope with its by now familiar contents at Om, and then—since no set of 'Chalak' Om chronicles is complete without this event—he fainted dead away on our modest Pepperfry rug (acquired third-hand).

We revived the man with a snifter of Old Monk rum which we always kept handy for these not infrequent occasions, and in a few minutes, all the dignitaries were seated, albeit—in view of the limited furniture in our humble abode—in a somewhat constricted manner, with the Prime Justice having to sit upon the Reverse Bank Governor's lap, and the Vigilante Commission Chief upon that of the Ballot Commission Head. (I myself stood on the Misinformation Commission Chief's toes, and made the most of the rare opportunity by shifting my weight from one leg to the other and pressing down as hard as I possibly could.)

Om addressed the assembly of dignitaries. "The whole idea was to strike terror in your hearts with the vague and ill-defined foreboding of which the envelope and its contents are a harbinger. You would be filled with even more terror if you knew the source and meaning of the warnings. It calls for some specialised knowledge of these matters to infer the source, and Maurya, R. T. anticipated, correctly, that you would consult me, and that I would be in possession of the requisite knowledge. You see, gentlemen, there is no new crime upon this earth. It is a common feature of every secret society to have its own convention of issuing warnings to its victims before it executes them. To the Chief of the country's premier snooping agency at least, I am moved to impart this advice: you really should be thoroughly acquainted, you know, with the latest updated version of Heckethon's classic on *Secret Societies of the World*. If you were, you would know that the National Self-serving Sect (NSS), which is the ideological mentor of our government, has a Monitoring and Retribution cell whose job it is to warn people holding public office to demit it, on pain of—", and here Om made a gesture by drawing his forefinger across his throat. "The warning is typically delivered in a sealed, hand-delivered envelope containing that folded message you have seen and five amla seeds. The 'ψ' is the trademark signature, signifying the trident, of the Monitoring and Retribution Cell of the NSS."

"But why are we being asked to step down? We have, after all, been loyal to the ruling dispensation!"

"Quite," said Om, knowingly. "That is everywhere in evidence. But possibly not loyal enough, especially considering that loyalties can be—ah—switched with elections looming on the horizon. As to what you do next—step down or stay on—well, that is entirely up to you." 'Chalak' Om shrugged his shoulders indifferently, presented the dignitaries with his bill, and signalled that the consultation was over.

After I had seen the last of them off, I returned to my chair and said: "Well, Om, what will they do? Resign or stay on? And if they resign, by whom will they be replaced?"

"Of course they will resign, Vatsan: they have always had a proper regard for their health. As to who will replace them, you should have no difficulty in anticipating if you were familiar with my monograph *On the One-Hundred-and-Thirty-two Varieties of Godman, Guru and Sage, with Specific Reference to the Distinctive Differences and Essential Sameness of Their Devices, Schemes and Stratagems*. The field is presently bristling with competitors, but the most likely candidate, by my reckoning, is—" and here Om mentioned a name.

He was to be proved right, of course. The foregoing account will have enabled the reader to learn how as many as seven of this country's major institutions—the Apex Court, the Reverse Bank, the Media Trust, the Misinformation Commission, the Vigilante Commission, the Ballot Commission, and the Central Snooping Bureau—came to be headed by a single personage who earned the sobriquet of "Seven-in-One and All-in-All": Yogi Swamy Sadguru Baba Sri Sri Mahamahopadhyaya Parabrahma Brahmaccharya Vedanti – III.

The adventure of the distinguished visitors

It was often remarked by even the foremost experts in the field of forensic crime that when it comes to the challenge posed by that category of offence which is constituted by seemingly insoluble mysteries, the final

court of appeal was always Mr 'Chalak' Om. When the official police force, and criminal detective agencies (private or public), had drawn a blank and admitted to bafflement over a case, it was customary to turn to Om for what was commonly acknowledged as the last and only source of assistance left in the matter of shining a light on the dark shrouds of mystery in which the case was enveloped. A corollary view was that if there was something one could get past 'Chalak' Om, it must be something one could get past anyone else. In the account that follows I present two examples of this proposition.

It was the year '19 in which the circumstances narrated here occurred. On the closing morning of one of the severest January winters which the capital city had witnessed in a long time, our landlady had just cleared away the remnants of our breakfast, Om had lighted up the first of the Langar Chhap *bidi* stubs he had smoked the previous night, and I had opened the latest issue of the *Vyapam Journal of Medical Malpractice*, when we heard the sound of steps upon the stair, followed by a peal on the doorbell of our humble abode at b122 Bekar Street.

I opened the door to admit three gentlemen with bald heads, dark glasses on their noses, and mufflers concealing the lower halves of their respective faces. It was revealed in a moment that our visitors were the Union Minister of Unlawful Activities and two of his Departmental Chiefs—the Chief of the Bureau of Unaccounted Wealth (BUW) and the Chief of the Directorate of Dodgy Statistics (DDS). We were informed that they did not wish to be known to be consulting 'Chalak' Om, and were consequently travelling *incognito* in their unobtrusive disguise of skull-caps, dark goggles, and layers of muffler.

The BUW Chief wished to know what Om made of the recently conducted demonetisation exercise, while the DDS Chief wondered what Om made of the government's promise to double farmer incomes in five years. These struck me as somewhat odd questions to address to a consulting detective. Om, however, was at his charming best, and in a matter of a few minutes, he had managed to get rid of our visitors through a bland mixture of non-committal views, inconsequential suggestions, and diversionary conversation.

When our visitors had departed, I said: "What was all that about, Om?"

Om allowed himself a hearty chuckle before responding: "The fellows were here to pick my brain and to test the water, my dear Vatsan. They wished to employ me as a guinea-pig for judging the outcome of how well they might have succeeded in bluffing the world at large with their promises of mopping up black money through demonetisation and relieving agrarian distress by doubling farmer incomes."

"Speaking of demonetisation," said I, "is there any aspect of that phenomenon to which you might wish to draw my attention?"

"To the curious aspect of the missing 1000 and 500 rupee currency notes."

"But, if I have got it right, the value of these currency notes in circulation was estimated at Rs. 15.41 lakh crore before demonetisation, and something like Rs. 15.31 lakh crore was returned in less than two years after demonetisation: there *are* no missing currency notes to speak of!"

"That," remarked Om, "is the curious aspect."

"But how does one explain it?"

"Ah! There's the wonder of it! All of the black money held in the denominations in question has been laundered and re-injected into the system. Behind the 'purification' is a single criminal master-mind—I call him the Chandragupta of Crime—who presides like a great big malevolent spider at the centre of a web over countless criss-crossing networks of deceit, intrigue, treachery, violence, and sharp practice. There is not a *havala* deal, not a case of over-invoicing of imports or under-invoicing of exports, not a shady transaction in real estate or mining or education, not an illicit off-shore expatriation of funds—not a single one of these activities of which he is unaware or in which, indeed, he is uninvolved. He uses the powers-that-be, even as they use him, in a symbiotic relationship of mutual benefit and favour."

"Who *is* this man, Om?"

"His name is Raj Tungesh Maurya, or Professor Maurya, R. T., as he calls himself. He is a brilliant scientist, a former Professor of Mathematical Anatomy, who wrote a tract titled the *Schematics of an Adenoid*, and whose work on the Trinomial Theorem enjoyed a substantial sub-continental vogue. It is not without reason that the Ministry of Unlawful Activities is interested in divining what, if anything, I know of Maurya, R. T. What the fellows are ignorant of is that I am hard upon the tracks of this consummate villain, and it is only a matter of time before he falls into my grasp." Om had a faraway look in his eyes; and I was not to know until later that his plans would find their culmination in an event I have recorded elsewhere under the heading of "The Adventure of the Final Problem."

"As for the other question, Om," said I. "How will they double farmer incomes?"

"*They* won't. They have hired econometricians—as Martin Gardner would call them—who will do the job for them by massaging the data and employing advanced Economicstricks techniques of manipulation. That is how they have estimated the figures on growth of per capita income, and how one of them has inflated the economy's net employment figures."

"But still: doubling farmer incomes! How can that possibly be accomplished?"

"Do not forget that the guiding light in these matters—Maurya, R. T.—is a mathematician. Farmer incomes will be doubled by subjecting them to a positive homogeneous linear transformation."

"Meaning?"

"Meaning multiplying the income data by two. Now I suggest we do that to a glass of rum from this bottle of Export Quality alcohol which I have succeeded in—ah—abstracting from the capacious overcoat pocket of the BUW Chief who doubtless receives regular consignments of the stuff from some Liquor Baron or other. Will you do the honours, Vatsan?"

"With pleasure, my dear Om, with pleasure!"

There are those who might call him anti-national, but 'Chalak' Om is as wholly Indian at heart as anybody could possibly wish. We clinked our glasses, and my friend rounded off the evening with an impromptu little rendering on his fiddle of a favourite tune from—appropriately enough—that old and well-loved film *Shri 420*:

Mera juta hai jaapaani, ye patloon inglistaani
Sar pe laal topi rusi, phir bhi dil hai hindustaani!

Index

absconding defaulters, adventure 68–70
'Adventure of the Sealed Room, The' (Doyle) 26
adventures: absconding defaulters 68–70; of 'Chalak' Om 63–80; of distinguished visitors 76–80; of five amla seeds 74–76; of vanished governor 65–67
Agee, James 10
agents provocateurs 41
āhūtaprapalāyinvijñāna 60
American Idol 50
American War of Independence 8
amla seeds, adventure 74–76
anarchists 32
Arrow, Kenneth J. 1, 5–7, 15, 24; brief commemoration of 5–7; work in economics 5–7
Arrow-Chenery-Minhas-Solow Production Function 5
Arrow-Debreu contingent markets 29
Arrow-Debreu Model of General Equilibrium 5
Arrow Impossibility Theorem 5
Arrow Model of Health Insurance and Market Failure 5
Arrow-Pratt Measures of Risk-Aversion 5
Arrow's Extended Sympathy 5
Atkinson, Anthony B. 1, 5–7; brief commemoration of 5–7; work in economics 5–7

Bālakarmanvidohakalā 60
Banach spaces 31
bankruptcy 35, 37

Basu, Kaushik 45
Becker, Gary 21
beggary 22
Bengal Famine 18–19
Bentham, Jeremy 9, 33
blackmail 22
Blinder, Alan 21
'Blue Cross, The' (Chesterton) 22
Bossert-Pfingsten restriction 32
Bradman, Don 18, 34
Brahmananda, P. R. 7
brushing teeth, economics of 21
budgetary allocations 11
Bulldog Drummond 25
burglary 22
Burke, Edmund 9

Cardus, Neville 33
'Case of Identity, The' (Doyle) 22
'Chalak' Om, adventures of 63–80
'Charles Augustus Milverton' (Doyle) 22
Chesterton, G. K. 22, 25
child-work 60
Citizens of India 61
Coase Theorem 33
Cobb-Douglas production process 30
Commission on Global Poverty 7
communal majoritarianism 2
competitive equilibrium 15
Compton, Denis 18, 34
Convex Utility Function (CUF) Theorem 31
counterfeiting 22
Creasy, John 23

Index

cricket Test match 18
Crispin, Edmund 25

dancing men, return of 70–74
Daridrabhūmicauryavṛttiśāstra 60
'Death in the Excelsior' (Wodehouse) 25
Death in the Excelsior and Other Stories (Wodehouse) 25
de Mandeville, Bernard 16
demonetisation 60
Dickson Carr, John 25
disciplinary parochialism 2
Disqualifying Legislators see Lokatantravipralambhana (The Frauds of Democracy)
distinguished visitors, adventure 76–80
Dodgson, Charles Lutwidge 24
'Dog College' 23
dominant strategy 17
Doyle, Arthur Conan 22, 24–26
Dresher, Melvin 17

Economic and Political Weekly 34
economics 29–39; cricket as game 33–34; imperium of 38–39; of incentives 37–38; inequality, understanding 32; justice for all 61; of land acquisition 32–33; Leacockian view of 48–56; learning 59–62; music and 30–31; open economy, inflation 29–30; poor are profligate 31; prologue 61–62; subsidies 34–35; taxes 36–37; themes 13–20
economist's descent: crime 21–26; fiction and economics of crime 21–23; Locked-Room Mysteries, attractions 23–26; profit motive 21–23
efficiency 13
'Engineer's Thumb, The' (Doyle) 22
entitlement-failure 18–19
entitlements 18; theory of famines 20
equitableness 13, 15
esoteric theories 1
Evening Standard 26
Exploits of Sherlock Holmes, The 26

Fable of the Bees, The, or, Private Vices, Publick Benefits (de Mandeville) 16

fairness 13
famine: classic indictments 18–20; phenomenon 1
Fen, Gervase 25
First Theorem of Welfare Economics 15
Flood, Merrill 17
'Flying Stars, The' (Chesterton) 22
'Food Availability Decline' 18–19
Frankfurt, Harry 51
Franklin, Benjamin 9
French Revolution 8, 9

gamakaas 30
game theory 1, 16–18
General Competitive Analysis 5
General Competitive Equilibrium 16
General Equilibrium Theory 15
General Theory of Employment, Interest and Money (Keynes) 60
global financial crisis 14
global poverty line 40–47, 51
Gödel, Kurt 24
Goebbels, Joseph 60
goods-and-services-taxation 60
Granger-causality 30
Great Leap Forward 18
Great Poverty Escape Act 50
Gulliver's Travels (Swift) 19

Hahn, Frank 5–7, 15, 22, 38
Hayloft, Hezekiah 54–56
Heckethon, C. W. 76
Heller, Joseph 17
Henry, O. 23
hermeneutic interpretability 62
heterogeneities 44
Holmes, Sherlock 24–26; stories 22
homo economicus 21
Hornung, E. W. 22
Hound of the Baskervilles, The (Doyle) 22
Human Capital School 21
Human Capital Theory 21
humane scepticism 2
human trafficking 54
'Hunchback Cat, The' (Crispin) 25

impersonation 22
Impossibility Theorem 24
incentive compatibility 23

incentives 37–38
Innocence of Father Brown, The (Chesterton) 25
Invisible Hand 14–16

Jain, Satish 15
Jefferson, Thomas 9

Kaisiki Nishada 30
Kaplan, Hyman 40–47
Kerala Mathematical School 60
Keynes, John Maynard 60
kidnapping and ransom 23
Kleene, S. C. 31
Kolm, Serge-Christophe 6
Komal Dhaivat 30
Komal Rishabh 30

La Fayette 9
land acquisition 32–33, 60
Land Acquisition Bill 32
Laughing Gas (Wodehouse) 23
Leacockian view, economics today 48–56; conjurer's revenge 50–52; hero in homespun 54–56; Hezekiah Hayloft, life struggle 54–56; maddened by mystery 48–50; psupernatural, psychic pstory of 52–54
Leibnitz, Gottfried 60
Little Nugget, The (Wodehouse) 23
Locked-Room Mysteries, attractions of 23–26
Lokatantravipralambhana (The Frauds of Democracy) 60
lore 13–14

Madhyamavati 30
Magna Carta 10
majority voting 24
manodharmic kalpanaswaras 31
'Man with the Twisted Lip, The' (Doyle) 22
market 13–15
market-driven capitalist economies 14
'Market Failures: Almost Always?' (Mukherjee) 15
Maurya, Raj Tungesh 79
Meier, Ernst Heinrich 60
Meta-Mathematics (Kleene) 31

missing aircraft case 63–65
'Modest Proposal, A' (Swift) 19
Mohana Kalyani 30
monetary sterilization 29
money-metric poverty simpliciter 46
Moonstone, The (Collins) 22
Mukherjee, Anjan 15
murder for inheritance 22
'Mystery of the Slip-Coach, The' (Sapper) 25

Naoroji, Dadabhai 1, 19, 20
Nash Equilibrium 17–18, 34, 55
nationalistic chauvinism 2
National Self-serving Sect (NSS) 76
Newton, Isaac 60

On Bullshit (Frankfurt) 51
'On the Measurement of Inequality' (Atkinson) 6
'On the Measurement of Poverty' (Atkinson) 6

Paine, Tom 1, 8–12; budgetary calculations 12; query 12
Pareto efficiency 14–15
parliamentary democracy 10
parochial appropriation 42
penmanship 62
petitioner's claim 61
Plumstead Radical Club, London 20
political economy 37
political philosophy 9
Poor Laws of England 12
Poor Taxes 12
Poverty and Famines (Sen) 18
Poverty and Un-British Rule in India (Naoroji) 19
Praja Sampoorna-nāśa Prakarana 60
Prati Madhyama 30
Principia Mathematica 24
Prisoner's Dilemma 16–17
private egotism 14–15
private greed 22, 38
private rationality 14, 22, 38
private-sector banks 13
public morality 9
public-sector banks 13
Public Transport Corporation (PTC) 14

84 Index

'radical' *force majeure* 31
Ramsey-Euler problem 30
'Ransom of Red Chief, The' (Henry) 23
rational agent 15
Reflections on the Revolution of France (Burke) 9
Return of Sherlock Holmes, The (Doyle) 73
Rights of Man (Paine) 1, 8–12; social security and skewed priorities 11–12
right-wing religious extremism 2
Robinson, Joan 6
Ronald Standish (Sapper) 25

Sankarabharanam 30
Second Theorem of Welfare Economics 15
'Secret Garden, The' (Chesterton) 25
Secret Societies of the World (Heckethon) 76
self-interest 14
Selten-Harsyani equilibria 37
Sen, Amartya 18, 20, 43, 44–45
Shuddha Gandhar 30
Sign of Four, The (Doyle) 22
'Silver Blaze' (Doyle) 22
Smith, Adam 14, 16
Social Choice Theory 23–24
social sector spending 12
social security 11–12
'Speckled Band, The' (Doyle) 24–25
Spilrajn's theorem 30
Sraffa, Piero 6

'Stockbroker's Clerk, The' (Doyle) 22
Strand Magazine 24–25
subsidies 34–35
Summer Game, The (Cardus) 33
Swift, Jonathan 1, 19, 20

Tarnova, Olga 41
tax concessions 11
taxes 36–37
Templar, Simon 23
'Three Garridebs, The' (Doyle) 22
Trinomial Theorem 79
Tucker, Albert 17

Utilitarianism 9

vanished governor, adventure of 65–67
vedanomics 59–60
Vitathavādin 60
Vyapam Journal of Medical Malpractice 78

Washington, George 9
Wealth of Nations, The (Smith) 16
Welfare Economics 15
welfare state 11; foundations 8–12
Wikipedia 6
Wodehouse, P. G. 23, 25
writ of *certiori* 56
writ of *mandamus* 56

Yeats, William Butler 6, 15